A THEORY OF PARODY

A THEORY
OF PARODY

THE TEACHINGS OF TWENTIETH-CENTURY ART FORMS

LINDA HUTCHEON

METHUEN

New York and London

First published in 1985 by
Methuen, Inc.
29 West 35th Street, New York, NY 10001
Reprinted 1986

Published in Great Britain by
Methuen & Co. Ltd
11 New Fetter Lane, London EC4P 4EE

Printed in Great Britain
at the University Printing House,
Cambridge

Library of Congress Cataloging in Publication Data
Hutcheon, Linda, 1947-
    A theory of parody.

    Bibliography: p.
    Includes index.
    1. Arts, Modern — 20th century.   2. Aesthetics,
Modern — 20th century.   3. Parody in art.   4. Parody.
I. Title.
NX650.P37H87   1984   700'.1   84-14856
ISBN 0-416-37080-2
ISBN 0-416-37090-X (pbk.)

British Library Cataloguing in Publication Data
Hutcheon, Linda
    A theory of parody.
    1. Parody in art — History — 20th century
    2. Arts, Modern — 20th century
    I. Title
    700'.9'04   NX650.P37

ISBN 0-416-37080-2
ISBN 0-416-37090-X Pbk

CONTENTS

LIST OF ILLUSTRATIONS

ACKNOWLEDGMENTS

One of the very real pleasures of working on such a broad topic as this for so many years is the number of people with whom I have come into contact who share an interest in and enthusiasm for parody in some form or other. For their own inspiring work in this area and for their invaluable responses to my own efforts, I should like to thank Daniel Bilous, University of Constantine, Algeria; Clive Thomson and the "Groupar" of Queen's University, Kingston; Bernard Andrès and the 1982 Séminaire Intersémiotique at the Université du Québec à Montréal; Michael Riffaterre and Gérard Genette at the 1981 poetics colloquium at Columbia University; the participants in the 1984 ISISSS; and, closer to home, my friends Magdalene Redekop, University of Toronto, Douglas Duncan and Mary O'Connor, McMaster University, Hamilton. I am also grateful to those who helped me by passing on their favorite parodies: Deborah Lebaron, Jim Brasch, Joann Bean, Alison Lee, Geert Lernout and many others. A debt is also owed, on a more general level, to the interest and advice of friends and colleagues: Gabriel Moyal, Janet Paterson, Laurel Braswell, Ron Vince. To Janice Price and her anonymous, acute readers at Methuen go the sincerest thanks any author could offer. And, as always, it is my husband, Michael, who deserves not only my gratitude for his continued supportive encouragement, but also the credit for being the most analytic and provocative sounding-board and critic one could ever wish for.

Many audiences over the last five or six years have heard isolated ideas from this book in their first, tentative formulations. For giving me the opportunity to thrash out my theory in a public forum, I should like to express my thanks to the following institutions: Columbia University, the Centro Internazionale di Semiotica e Linguistica (Urbino), Queen's

University, McGill University, State University of New York at
Binghamton, Université du Québec à Montréal, University of Toronto
French Department, University of Ottawa, University of Western
Ontario, McMaster University, and the Toronto Semiotic Circle. I am
particularly indebted to the audience responses at these talks, and at the
1982 International Comparative Literature Association Conference, the
1980 and 1981 meetings of the Modern Language Association of
America, the 1980 gathering of the members of the Canadian Semiotics
Association, the 1983 sessions of the Canadian Comparative Literature
Association, and the 1984 meeting of ACUTE.

Similarly, over the years, some of the ideas in the book appeared in
very different form, context, and sometimes even language in a number
of journals *(Poétique, Diacritics, Texte, The Canadian Review of Comparative
Literature)*. Few of the ideas will probably be recognizable in their
subsequent development here, although Figures 1 and 2 are reproduced,
in English, from *Poétique*, 46 (avril 1981).

The author and publisher would like to thank Faber & Faber Ltd for
permission to quote a poem from *Making Cocoa for Kingsley Amis* by
Wendy Cope.

Toronto, 1984   LINDA HUTCHEON incipit parodia

Nietzsche

1

INTRODUCTION

We are backward-looking explorers and parody is the central
expression of our times. *Dwight Macdonald*

As the title of this book indicates, this is a study of the implications for
theory of modern artistic practice. Parody is not a new phenomenon
by any means, but its ubiquity in all the arts of this century has seemed
to me to necessitate a reconsideration of both its nature and its function. The "postmodern" world, as Lyotard (1979) calls our postindustrial
developed West, may well be suffering today from a lack of faith in
systems requiring extrinsic validation. But this has been true of the entire
century. Art forms have increasingly appeared to distrust external
criticism to the extent that they have sought to incorporate critical commentary within their own structures in a kind of self-legitimizing short-
circuit of the normal critical dialogue. In other fields – from linguistics
to scientific philosophy – the question of self-reference has also become
the focus of attention. The modern world seems fascinated by the ability
of our human systems to refer to themselves in an unending mirroring
process. For instance, inspired by mathematical logic, computer systems,
the drawings of Escher, the paintings of Magritte, and the music of Bach,
Douglas Hofstadter's (1979) book, *Gödel, Escher, Bach: An Eternal
Golden Braid*, has studied and indeed taught us the mechanics that allow
systems to refer to and reproduce themselves. Even scientific knowledge
today seems characterized by the inevitable presence within itself of some
discourse on its own validating principles. The omnipresence of this
metadiscursive level has prompted some observers to posit a general
concept of performance that would serve to explain the self-reflexiveness
of all cultural forms – from television commercials to movies, from music
to fiction.

It is in the context of this general modern interrogation of the nature of self-reference and legitimacy that comes the contemporary interest in parody, the genre that has been described as both a symptom and a critical tool of the modernist episteme (Rose 1979). Certainly parodic texts have been used as models by the Russian formalists, and, of course, *Don Quijote* is the work that best reveals, according to Foucault (1970), the separation between the modern and Renaissance epistemes. From Pound and Eliot through to contemporary performance artists and Post-Modern architects, intertextuality and auto-representation have come to dominate critical attention. With this focus has come an aesthetic of process, of the dynamic activity of the perception, interpretation, and production of works of art (or texts, as I shall refer to them here).

Many eras have vied for the title of the "Age of Parody." Certainly the nineteenth-century infatuation with specific and occasional parody of Romantic and late Romantic poems and novels provided a source of contemporary opinion on a major literary movement (Priestman 1980). The mixture of praise and blame makes such parody into a critical act of reassessment and acclimatization. Since this period had a literate, middle-class reading public, parodists could venture beyond using canonic familiar texts (the Bible, the classics) to include the contemporary. But parody in the twentieth century has gone beyond this conservative function of keeping modishness in line. Unlike Dryden or even J. K. Stephen, T. S. Eliot seemed to feel that he might not be able to trust in his readership's knowledge – the knowledge necessary to understand his allusive or parodic poetry – but he would force his reader to work towards regaining the Western literary heritage (and some of the Eastern as well) while reading *The Waste Land.* In other words, parody in this century is one of the major modes of formal and thematic construction of texts. And, beyond even this, it has a hermeneutic function with both cultural and even ideological implications.

Parody is one of the major forms of modern self-reflexivity; it is a form of inter-art discourse. We need only think of the work of novelists like Italo Calvino or John Fowles to see the most overt and explicit formulation of its nature and function in fiction. But, in other art forms, parody is just as important. Magritte's *The Treason of Images* or *This is not a Pipe* is, among many other things, a parody of the medieval and baroque emblem form: the picture, title, and motto, however, do not work towards their usual harmonious totality of meaning. (It was also intended as a rebuttal of Le Corbusier's use of a pipe as the symbol of plain functional design.) It was Magritte himself who saw the connection between his parodic contestation of earlier unproblematic forms and Michel Foucault's work on the relationships between words and things, between language and its referents. Foucault responded with a study (1983) of Magritte's transgression of the more general conventions of representation and reference in art. Adding another level of complexity to the game, Foucault appropriated Magritte's label for his own study. Now both have produced works that can be labeled "This is not a Pipe."

Music has shared with the other arts in this general turning inward to reflect upon its own constitution. According to some analysts, the main subject matter and source of interest of much contemporary music are its formal properties (Morgan 1977). A major way that music can comment upon itself from within (as opposed to relying on accounts of precompositional planning) is through parodic reworkings of previous music. Over twenty years ago, Edward Cone (1960) localized the challenge to traditional concepts and modes of musical analysis in his argument that modern music required that the analysis be determined by the object it purports to elucidate. In other words, the composition itself should be relied upon to reveal the methods of analysis needed for its comprehension. This is perhaps even more evident in metafictional works of literature which include or constitute their own first critical commentary (see Hutcheon 1980).

I too believe that any consideration of modern parody at the theoretical level must be governed by the nature and function of its manifestations in actual works of art. I would like to reverse, in other words, the Russian formalist practice. For Šklovskij, *Tristram Shandy*, *Don Quijote*, and *Don Juan* were prized because their parodic form coincided with his own theory of the essential conventionality of literary form and the role of parody in its denuding or laying bare (Erlich 1955, 1965, 193). I want to start, instead, with the fact of the presence and importance of modern parody, and work from there towards a theory that might best account for this phenomenon. One of the reasons for this strategy is that the art forms of our century have been extremely and self-consciously didactic, and seem to be getting more so. This study is a sort of plea to heed the teachings of art as well as criticism. We seem more willing to accept the latest theory, hot off the press, than to trust to the art itself. We prefer to leave to time and communal consensus the task of deciding which works merit our attention. This is often, however, less a question of evaluation than one of convenience. In changing the focus of attention from aesthetic merit (however determined) to instructional value, this study seeks to investigate the definition and functions of parody in modern art, and perhaps even to argue in its defense.

It has need of defenders. Parody has been called parasitic and derivative.

Leavis's famous distaste, not to say contempt, for parody was based on his belief that it was the philistine enemy of creative genius and vital originality (see Amis 1978, xv). These terms give a clue to the reasons for the denigration of a form that is pervasive in the art of our century. Some critics reject what they see as parody's superimposition of an external order upon a work that is presumed to be original (if it is to be valued) (Rovit 1963, 80). What is clear from these sorts of attacks is the continuing strength of a Romantic aesthetic that values genius, originality, and individuality. In such a context, parody must needs be considered at best a very minor form. However, since Eliot's valorization of the "historical sense" and the formalist (New Critical, structuralist) complementary, if very different, turning to the text, we have witnessed a renewed interest in questions of textual appropriation and even influence. Now, however, we see influence as a burden (Bate 1970) or as a cause of anxiety (Bloom 1973). Parody is one mode of coming to terms with the texts of that "rich and intimidating legacy of the past" (Bate 1970, 4). Modern artists seem to have recognized that change entails continuity, and have offered us a model for the process of transfer and reorganization of that past. Their double-voiced parodic forms play on the tensions created by this historical awareness. They signal less an acknowledgement of the "inadequacy of the definable forms" of their predecessors (Martin 1980, 666) than their own desire to "refunction" those forms to their own needs.

This more positive method of dealing with the past recalls in many ways the classical and Renaissance attitude to the cultural patrimony. For writers like Ben Jonson, it is clear that imitation of previous works was considered part of the labor of writing poetry. After being repressed by the Romantic or post-Enlightenment emphasis on the need for something else (genius, and so on), this stress on craft and knowledge of the past has come back into focus today. This is partly, I suspect, because so many artists are now part of the academy, but it is also probably a result of aesthetic formalism, from Roger Fry to Roland Barthes. Michel Foucault (1977, 115) has argued that the entire concept of artist or author as an original instigator of meaning is only a privileged moment of individualization in the history of art. In that light, it is likely that the Romantic rejection of parodic forms as parasitic reflected a growing capitalist ethic that made literature into a commodity to be owned by an individual. The last century saw the rise of copyright laws, of course, and with them came defamation suits against parodists. Perhaps this means that today's turning to parody reflects what European theorists see as a crisis in the entire notion of the subject as a coherent and continuous source of signification. Parody's overt turning to other art forms implicitly contests Romantic singularity and thereby forces a reassessment of the process of textual production.

The auto-reflexivity of modern art forms often takes the form of parody and, when it does so, it provides a new model for artistic process. In an effort to demystify the "sacrosanct name of the author" and to "desacralize the origin of the text," postmodernist critics and novelists like Raymond Federman (1977, 161) have argued for the complementarity of the acts of textual production and reception. The writer must "stand on equal footing with the reader/listener in an effort *to make sense* out of the language common to both of them." For some advocates of "plagiarism" or contextual free play, originality becomes the "hobgoblin of rigid egos": "each page is a field on which is inscribed the trace of every conceivable page recorded in the past or anticipated in the future" (Tatham 1977, 146). While parody offers a much more limited and controlled version of this activation of the past by giving it a new and often ironic context, it makes similar demands upon the reader, but these are demands more on his or her knowledge and recollection than on his or her openness to play. Perhaps it is true that all avant-garde texts have been, in Laurent Jenny's words, "volontiers savant" (deliberately and willingly learnèd) (1976, 279), haunted by cultural memories whose tyrannical weight they must overthrow by their incorporation and inversion of them.

It will be clear by now that what I am calling parody here is not just that ridiculing imitation mentioned in the standard dictionary definitions. The challenge to this limitation of its original meaning, as suggested (as we shall see) by the etymology and history of the term, is one of the lessons of modern art that must be heeded in any attempt to work out a theory of parody that is adequate to it. Joyce's *Ulysses* provides the most blatant example of the difference in both scope and intent of what I shall label as parody in the twentieth century. There are extended parallels with the Homeric model on the level of character and plot, but these are parallels with an ironic difference: Molly/Penelope, waiting in her insular room for her husband, has remained anything but chaste in his absence. Like Eliot's ironic echoes of Dante and many others in his poetry, this is not just a structural inversion; it also signals a change in what used to be called the "target" of parody. While the *Odyssey* is clearly the formally backgrounded or parodied text here, it is not one to be mocked or ridiculed; if anything, it is to be seen, as in the mock epic, as an ideal or at least as a norm from which the modern departs. This is not to say that there have not been modern heirs to Calverley and Squire, writers of what is more traditionally seen as parody. We need only recall the work of Max Beerbohm or even Pound's "Winter is icummen in." In fact, what is remarkable in modern parody is its range of intent – from the ironic and playful to the scornful and ridiculing.

Parody, therefore, is a form of imitation, but imitation characterized by ironic inversion, not always at the expense of the parodied text. Max Ernst's *Pietà* is an Oedipal inversion of Michelangelo's sculpture: a petrified father holds a living son in his arms, replacing the living mother and her dead son, Christ. Parody is, in another formulation, repetition with critical distance, which marks difference rather than similarity. In this it goes beyond mere allusive variation such as in the *honkadori* technique in Japanese court poetry, which echoes past works in order to borrow a context and to evoke an atmosphere (Brower and Miner 1961, 14-15). The ironic inversion of Dante's *Commedia* by Pound's *Hugh Selwyn Mauberley* (1928, 171-87) is more to the point. Here the parody lies in the differences between the personal, aesthetic, and moral journeys of two exiles. Dante's dignity is replaced by Mauberley's self-pity; his involvement with the political reality of Florence is contrasted to the aesthete's self-willed alienation. Instead of inheriting a long tradition of classical, Italian, and Provençal poetry, Mauberley has only the nineties' decadence. The concrete materiality of Dante's descriptions even of things supernatural is replaced by the "obscure reveries / of the inward gaze." As Dante moves out of himself to beauty and finally to God in an act of spiritual fulfilment, the modern journey leads only to the inner ego, to the failure of love, to "subjective hosannah," and to the inadequacies of the flesh. In Pound's poem, the imagery (of eyes, mouth, and so on) is the same as in Dante's, but the context is inverted. The same characters are mentioned and the same moral stance suggested, but the relations to them are ironically different. Instead of an acceptance and use of the past for new creation, Mauberley seeks to deny the social and aesthetic tradition that would give his life and work meaning (see Malkoff 1967).

Ironic inversion is a characteristic of all parody: think of Byron's *Don Juan*'s reversal of the legend (the women here chase after him) and of the conventions of the epic. Similarly, criticism need not be present in the form of ridiculing laughter for this to be called parody. Euripides was considered to have parodied Aeschylus and Sophocles when, in his *Medea*, he replaced the traditional male protagonist with a woman, and a woman who was an outsider rather than a member of a Greek family of renown. The female Corinthian chorus replaced the elders of state and the suppliants, yet, with added irony, they also support Medea in her hatred of Corinth. The male hero turns out to be base – hypocritical and shallow. Although bloodied by four murders, Medea is saved by the gods. This is the same kind of inversion we find in Pound or in a contemporary film such as Peter Greenaway's *The Draughtsman's Contract*.

In its attention to visual and verbal detail, this film is a loving parody of eighteeth-century painting and Restoration comedy. It is a parody and not an imitation because of what Greenaway does to the conventions of the form. First of all, they are superimposed upon the seemingly very different conventions of the murder mystery, and then both are inserted into a metadiscursive context focused on the representation of reality. As the "hero" sketches a country house, its owner is murdered, and clues (in the form of items of his clothing) are integrated into the accurate, realistic drawings. The framing device which the artist, Mr Neville, employs in his drawing is frequently both used and mirrored by the camera, which composes scenes like paintings. The black and white of the drawings contrasts with the lush color of the film, but this contrast serves only to signal a second function of the color opposition, one that coincides with the conventions, not to say clichés, of all moral drama wherein black signifies evil and white denotes innocence. In this film, the traditional male sexual supremacy of Restoration comedy with which the plot begins is inverted in the second half, as the women take control of his sexual activities for their own purposes. It is totally *sub*verted at the end when the female plotters are replaced by the males who put the artist to death. The arrogant and manipulative Mr Neville is portrayed at the beginning dressed in black, making black marks on his white sheets of paper; his innocent female victims are clothed in white. The irony of this coding becomes clear by the end as we realize the superior manipulation of the women in white, and indeed as the film progresses the colors are reversed, ostensibly because the women are now in mourning. In reality, their true colors, so to speak, finally show, and the truly innocent Neville is dressed in white, a lamb ready for the slaughter. This ironic playing with multiple conventions, this extended repetition with critical difference, is what I mean by modern parody.

When Eliot gives Marvell's poetry a new context (or "trans-contextualizes" it), or when Stockhausen quotes but alters the melodies of many different national anthems in his *Hymnen*, parody becomes what one critic calls a productive-creative approach to tradition (Siegmund-Schultze 1977). In Stockhausen's words, his intent was "to hear familiar, old, preformed musical material with new ears, to penetrate and transform it with a musical consciousness of today" (cited in Grout 1980, 748). Similarly, the Brotherhood of Ruralists, whose very name suggests their admiration for the Pre-Raphaelite Brotherhood, overtly borrow and recontextualize compositional elements from earlier English landscape artists like Samuel Palmer. Graham Arnold's parodically entitled series *Harmonies poétiques et religieuses* is a homage to Ruskin, Jefferies, and T. S. Eliot that combines painting with a collage of photos, bits of music scores, and actual physical parts of the English countryside (an ear of corn, for instance). Quotation or borrowing like this is not meant to signal only similarity (cf. Altmann 1977). It is not a matter of nostalgic imitation of past models; it is a stylistic confrontation, a modern recoding which establishes difference at the heart of similarity. No integration into a new context can avoid altering meaning, and perhaps even value (Vodička 1964, 80). George Rochberg's Third String Quartet appropriates the conventions of an earlier period and gives them a new meaning. The third movement sounds like a set of variations by Beethoven, but we cannot analyze it as such. Its real significance lies in how it does *not* sound like Beethoven, because we know it was written in the 1970s: "Tonality simply cannot mean today what it did 150 years ago; it has a totally different relationship not only to the composer and listener but to the entire musical culture within whose context the piece exists and is experienced" (Morgan 1977, 50). In his famous essay, "The Literature of Exhaustion," John Barth (1967) remarked that, if Beethoven's Sixth Symphony were composed today, it would be an embarrassment – unless it were done ironically to show that the composer was aware of where music both is and has been.

The fact that I have been using examples from different art forms should make clear my belief that parody in non-literary works is not just a transfer from the practice of literature, as Bakhtin, however, claimed it was (1978, 229-33). Its frequency, prominence, and sophistication in the visual arts, for example, are striking. It is part of a move away from the tendency, within a Romantic ideology, to mask any sources by cunning cannibalization, and towards a frank acknowledgement (by incorporation) that permits ironic commentary. This is a version of what Leo Steinberg calls "inter-art traffic" (1978, 21). The most parodied paintings are, not surprisingly, the most familiar ones: the *Mona Lisa*, the *Last Supper*, the works of Picasso, and those of Vermeer (by George Deem, Malcolm Morley, James McGarrell, Carole Caroompas, and others). Parodic "trans-contextualization" can take the form of a literal incorporation of reproductions into the new work (by Joseph Cornell, Audrey Flack, Josef Levi, Sante Graziani) or of a reworking of the formal elements: for instance, Arakawa's parody of da Vinci's *Last Supper* is entitled *Next to the Last*, referring to the last preparatory drawing before

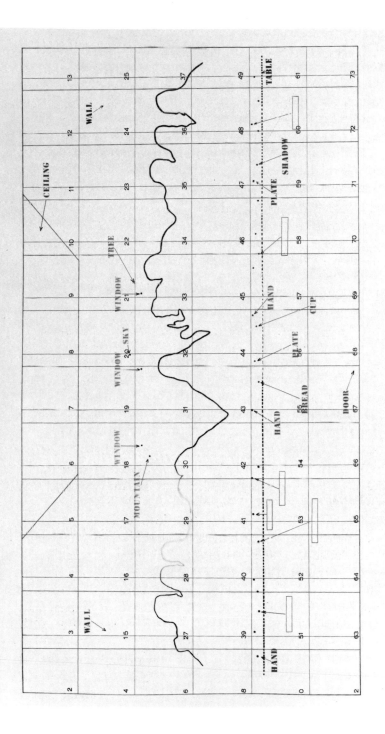

1 Shusaku Arakawa, *Next to the Last*, 1971

the painting, as well as to the work itself. The composition is squared out, the figures are silhouetted, as in a sketch, and some elements are labeled rather than drawn in (hand, cup). Such parody intends no disrespect, while it does signal ironic difference. It is one of the forms of what the 1978 exhibit at the Whitney Museum of American Art in New York called "Art about Art" (Lipman and Marshall 1978). Such art could almost be considered self-parodic in that it calls into question not only its relation to other art but its own identity. Self-parody in this sense in not just an artist's way of disowning earlier mannerisms by externalizations (as with Coleridge's "On a Ruined Cottage in a Romantic Country" or Swinburne's "Nephelidia"). It is a way of creating a form out of the questioning of the very act of aesthetic production (Poirier 1968, 339; cf. Stackelberg 1972, 162).

In my focus on twentieth-century art forms, I hope to suggest that there are probably no transhistorical definitions of parody possible. Nevertheless, I shall constantly be using examples from other periods to show that there are common denominators to all definitions of parody in all ages – although they are *not* the ones usually cited. It is modern parodic usage that is forcing us to decide what it is that we shall call parody today. In fact the closest model to present practice was not called parody at all, but imitation. I am thinking of the central and pervasive force of Renaissance imitation as what Thomas Greene calls a percept and an activity which "embraced not only literature but pedagogy, grammar, rhetoric, esthetics, the visual arts, music, historiography, politics and philosophy" (1982, 1). I am not claiming that modern parody is only Renaissance imitation: it would require the addition of an ironic and critical dimension of distanciation for it to be an accurate reflection of the art of today. But, like parody, imitation offered a workable and effective stance toward the past in its paradoxical strategy of repetition as a source of freedom. Its incorporation of another work as a deliberate and acknowledged construct is structurally similar to parody's formal organization. But the ironic distance of modern parody might well come from a loss of that earlier humanist faith in cultural continuity and stability that ensured the sharing of codes necessary to the comprehension of such doubly coded works. Imitation, however, offers a striking parallel to parody in terms of intent. In Greene's words: "Every creative imitation mingles filial rejection with respect, just as every parody pays its own oblique homage" (1982, 46).

With the eighteenth-century valorizing of wit and irony (Grannis 1931) came a move away from this idea of respect, except in the mock epic (which did not, in fact, mock the epic). The function of parody was often to be the malicious, denigrating vehicle of satire, a role it continues to play to this day in some forms of parody. Yet into the nineteenth century we find other persistent and extensive uses of parody, such as Jane Austen's (Moler 1968), which challenge the definition of parody as the conservative ridiculing of artistic fashion's extremes. Certainly the equivalent of the parodies of the Smith Brothers today would be the short, often satirical, parodies in *Punch* and other such magazines, but the more extended structural use of parody by Dickens in *Pickwick Papers* and Chesterton in *The Man that Was Thursday* is a closer model for the practice of novelists like Joyce and Mann, not to mention Barth and Banville. This is not to say that Christopher Ward's "The Dry Land," Samuel Hoffenstein's "The Moist Land," and Louis Untermeyer's "Einstein Among the Coffee Cups" are not parodies of Eliot's poetry. What I do want to suggest is that we must broaden the concept of parody to fit the needs of the art of our century – an art that implies another and somewhat different concept of textual appropriation. Certainly new directors like Robert Benton and Brian De Palma are not attempting to ridicule Hitchcock in films such as *Still of the Night* and *Blowout*. Often the works of the past become aesthetic models whose recasting in a modern work is frequently aimed at a satirical ridicule of contemporary customs or practices (Markiewicz 1967, 1265). The best historical model for this is the mock epic, as in *The Rape of the Lock* or the *Dunciad* with its use of Virgil's eclogues (Lawler 1974). Some critics have argued that the subplots in Elizabethan drama function in the same parodic fashion (Frye 1965).

Like all of these forms, and in contrast to those short, occasional parodies that were gathered into anthologies with such regularity in the late nineteenth and early twentieth centuries, the kind of parody upon which I wish to focus is an integrated structural modeling process of revising, replaying, inverting, and "trans-contextualizing" previous works of art. Perhaps the archetypal manifestation of this process is what is now called Post-Modern architecture. Since 1960, architects such as Paolo Portoghesi, Robert Venturi, Charles Moore, and others have self-consciously restored the idea of architecture as a dialogue with the past, as being doubly coded (Modern plus something else) or parodic. Eschewing the hermeticism and denial of function and relevance of High Modernism, these architects critically display an interest in historical memory and in codes of communication (Jencks 1980b, 13). This is not very different in either intent or structure from Iris Murdoch's modern inversions of earlier texts, her reworking (in the light of the Sartrean image of petrification by the "regard" of the Other) of the tales of both the

Medusa and John the Baptist in her *A Severed Head*, for instance. In his recent novel, *The Name of the Rose*, Umberto Eco "trans-contextualizes" characters, plot details, and even verbal quotations from Conan Doyle's "The Hound of the Baskervilles" into a medieval world of monks and (literally) textual intrigue. His Sherlock Holmes is William of Baskerville; his narrating Watson is Adso, the scribe who frequently does not know what he recollects and records. In the context of medieval and modern semiotics, Eco's hero's first example of reasoning à la Holmes – in a situation out of Voltaire's *Zadig* – takes on new meaning; the work of the detective becomes an analogue for textual interpretation: both are active, constructive, and indeed more creative than true to fact. The deadly struggle over what turns out to be Aristotle's lost poetics of the comic provides the context for the attack, by the monk, Jorge of Borgos, on the propriety of laughter; Eco's other extended parodic context here is, of course, the work of Jorge Luis Borges. This complex novel also contains extended parodies of the *Coena cipriani*, of other art works (those of Breughel and Buñuel, to cite two that will give an idea of Eco's range), as well as many other literary works.

In music, what is commonly called quotation or borrowing has become a significant, self-conscious aesthetic device only in this century, though it existed before (Rabinowitz 1981, 206n). Just as Rochberg used Mozart and Mahler in his *Music for the Magic Theatre*, so Foss uses the Prelude of Bach's Violin Partita in E in his "Phorion" *(Baroque Variations)*, but his quotation is in fragmented form, offering an ironic, nightmarish world through distortion. This is not the same as Liszt's *Réminiscences de Don Juan*, which develops certain themes of *Don Giovanni*. Ironic "transcontextualization" is what distinguishes parody from pastiche or imitation. Modern jazz, for instance, is therefore probably not in itself parodic, though there do exist some parodies even in this, an art form that tends to take itself very seriously. It is interesting that it is often women (a rarity in the jazz scene) who are willing or able to create the necessary ironic distance: Carla Bley's amusing "Reactionary Tango" is one such example.

In the visual arts, parody can manifest itself in relation to either particular works or general iconic conventions. René Payant's (1979, 1980) semiotic studies of what he calls quotation in painting reveal the complexity of the intersection of, in his terms, intertextuality and intersubjectivity – that is, the complexity of the meeting of two texts combined with the meeting of a painter and a viewer. The work of Magritte provides a clear example of a parodic transgression of many levels of iconic norms that moves beyond mere quotation. His simplest and most overt parodies are those based on specific paintings: David's portrait of Madame Récamier becomes a portrait of a coffin. It is clear from Magritte's letters that the work of Manet and David represented to him the ultimate achievements of objective representation in art and, as such, could not be ignored (Magritte 1979). Indeed, they must, for him, be superseded. But Magritte's parodies also operate on other than direct iconic models. Paintings like the different versions of *The Human Condition* parody conventions of both art (the function of framing) and visual perception. Magritte's parody of the general conventions of reference as well as the specific ones of the emblem form that we investigated earlier inspired more than just Michel Foucault. David Hlynsky recently produced a holograph called *These are not the Pipes* which models itself – albeit ironically – on Magritte's (the work is indeed a representation of not one smoking pipe but of a number of plumbing pipes), but the visual illusion of holography (of three-dimensional space) ironically increases the intensity of the power of art's conventions of representation. A similar complexity is achieved in a different way by Peter Blake's parodic *On the Balcony*. The four children on the bench hold a postcard or reproduction of Manet's *Le balcon*, a picture from *Romeo and Juliet*, implying the famous balcony scene (there is also a pennant from Verona elsewhere), and two photos of the royal family. The cliché of the lovers on the balcony is re-echoed in the two doves outside the dovecote. This kind of complexity makes parody into a variation on what Gary Saul Morson (1981, 48-9) calls a "boundary work" or doubly decodable text, though these works are perhaps more accurately described as having multiple coding, especially since conventions as well as particular texts are often involved.

Sometimes, in fact, it is conventions *as well as* individual works that are parodied. For example, the New York artist Vito Acconci's 1973 *Runoff* is a parody of two different sets of conventions as well as one specific text. It challenges the bases of most performance art, but also aims particularly at Yves Klein's double and simultaneous performance of his *Monotone Symphone* (a string quartet played one note for the duration) and *Anthropometry*, in which the male artist directed nude female models to cover their bodies in paint and role about on or against blank canvas. Acconci, instead, rubs his own, unpainted, male body against a freshly painted wall. He not only thereby ironically inverts Klein's sexist control but also reverses the standard conventions of instrumentality of brush to canvas. Here the body is the canvas; the wall is the applicator (as he moves against it). In this way, Acconci also manages to parody what abstract expressionists like Jackson Pollock felt was the correct "investiture of the self" (Barber 1983-4, 37).

The work of Tom Stoppard would provide another example of the complexity of the modern phenomenon that I want to call parody. In *Rosencrantz and Guildenstern are Dead*, there is a tension between the text we know *(Hamlet)* and what Stoppard does to it. Whenever an event is directly taken from the Shakespearian model, Stoppard uses the original words. But he "trans-contextualizes" them through his addition of scenes that the Bard never conceived. This is not like Ionesco's total inversion of the diction and moral value of characters in his *Macbett*; Stoppard's intention is not as satiric as Ionesco's. The same is true in *Travesties*, but there is yet another level of complexity because, as its plural title suggests, not only is there more than one parody, but those texts parodied are themselves often parodies, especially *Ulysses* and *The Importance of Being Earnest*. Wilde's play parodies the literature of romance and the comedy of manners. What one critic has called its "queer double consciousness" (Foster 1956, 23) is really only its parodic double coding. In Stoppard's play, *The Importance of Being Earnest* is foregrounded both as a formal model and as a source of parodic play by the plot, which involves Joyce's production of it in Zürich. The baby switch in Wilde's play becomes appropriately and significantly inverted when Joyce's own parodic "Oxen of the Sun" text is switched for Lenin's plan for the revolution. We might also recall that in that section of *Ulysses*, in addition to the various famous stylistic parodies, Stephen ironically inverts the language and actions of the Last Supper and the mass (Bauerle 1967), in a manner similar to his usurpation of the language of the Creator to describe his induction into the priesthood of the eternal imagination in *A Portrait of the Artist as a Young Man*. In both cases he uses parody as much to resacralize as to desacralize, to signal the change in the locus of his allegiance. In some of the stories of *Dubliners*, Joyce uses the superimposing structure of parody to organize his plot (as in "Grace," with its echoes of the *Divine Comedy* and of Job (Boyle 1970)) or to comment ironically on implications of certain literary forms (as in "Clay," where the Dickensian optimistic style of *A Christmas Carol* contrasts ironically with the reality described (Easson 1970)).

Similarly, Magritte's coffin studies are more than just parodic play with single earlier paintings. His *Perspective* has a long and complex history that includes not just Manet's *Le balcon* but Matisse's *Porte-fenêtre à Collioure* (which voided Manet's scene of its people in another way, leaving only the door's form), and also Goya's *Majas on a Balcony* – a model of Manet's (see pp. 16-17). I would not want to argue that such complex parodic echoing is unique to the twentieth century. Clearly works such as Petronius' *Satyricon libri* parodied not only the Greek novel form in its frame and episodes but other diverse specific works as well (Courtney 1962, 86-7). Nevertheless, the number of modern works of art in many media that partake of this mode does make it important, if not unique, to this century. The music of Peter Maxwell Davies provides another good example. His *Antechrist* was inspired, he claimed, by fifteenth-century woodcut blocks on the subject and by his own opera, *Taverner*, but its form begins with a straight rendering of "Deo confitemini-Domino," a thirteenth-century motet, which is then broken down and superimposed on related plainsong fragments – which the new context turns ironically inside out. For Davies, this inversion is related to the late medieval techniques of transformation processes (canon, etc.). He began his *Missa super L'Homme Armé* as an exercise to complete an anonymous fifteenth-century mass on the popular song "L'Homme Armé," but, inspired by the structure of Joyce's "Cyclops" episode in *Ulysses* (with its interrupted tavern conversation and parodic stylistic changes), he chose instead to rework the material to reveal more unorthodox relationships between foregrounded and backgrounded material. On the cover of the Decca L'Oiseau-Lyre recording, he calls the finished product a "progressive splintering of what is extant of the fifteenth-century original, with magnification and distortion of each splinter through many varied stylistic 'mirrors,' finishing with a 'dissolution' of it in the last automatic piano section."

I want to argue for calling such complex forms of "trans-contextualization" and inversion by the name of parody. It is indeed a form of "artistic recycling" (Rabinowitz 1980, 241), but a very particular form with very complex textual intentionality. Robbe-Grillet's *The Erasers* is a parody of both *Oedipus Rex* and Bely's *St Petersburg* in its structure, but the functions of the two parodic strains are more difficult to specify. What seems certain is that they are not the same. I want to retain the term parody for this structural and functional relationship of critical revision, partly because I feel that a word like quotation is too weak and carries (etymologically and historically) none of those parodic resonances of distance and difference that we have found to be present in modern art's reference to its past. Quotation might do, in a very general way, if we were dealing only with the adoption of another work as a guiding structural principle (Weisgerber 1970), but even then its usefulness is limited. As we shall see in the next chapter, we need a term that will allow us to deal with the structural and functional complexity of the artistic works themselves. According to their teachings, parody can obviously be a whole range of things. It can be a serious criticism, not necessarily of the parodied text; it can be a playful, genial mockery of codifiable forms.

2 René Magritte,
Perspective
(Le balcon de Manet),
1950

Its range of intent is from respectful admiration to biting ridicule. Nietzsche (1920-9, 61), in fact, wondered what was Diderot's relation to Sterne's text in *Jacques le fataliste:* was it imitation, admiration, mockery?

While we need to expand the concept of parody to include the extended "refunctioning" (as the Russian formalists called it) that is characteristic of the art of our time, we also need to restrict its focus in the sense that parody's "target" text is always another work of art or, more generally, another form of coded discourse. I stress this basic fact throughout this book because even the best works on parody tend to confuse it with satire (Freund 1981, for instance), which, unlike parody, is both moral and social in its focus and ameliorative in its intention. This is not to say, as we shall see, that parody does not have ideological or even social implications. Parody can, of course, be used to satirize the reception or even the creation of certain kinds of art. (I am aware that this separation would break down in a deconstructionist perspective where there is no *hors-texte,* but such a view of textuality is not my immediate context in this study.)

3 Édouard Manet,
Le balcon

4 F.J. de Goya,
Majas on a Balcony

What, then, can be parodied? Any codified form can, theoretically, be treated in terms of repetition with critical distance (Abastado 1976, 17; Morson 1981, 107), and not necessarily even in the same medium or genre. Literature is famous for parodying non-literary discourse. *Pale Fire* plays with editorial commentary; *Tom Jones, Tristram Shandy,* and even *Finnegans Wake* undermine the conventions of scholarly annotation and footnotes (Benstock 1983). Borges's "Pierre Menard, Author of the Quixote" parodies, among other things, the genre of the biblio-bio-critical note on a writer. This cross-genre play is not only the province of literature: Woody Allen's *Zelig* is, among other things, a cinematic parody of the television documentary and movie newsreel. If there is no parodiable code, as might be the case in nonsense or extreme hermetic works, imitation may be possible, but not parody (Stewart 1978, 1979, 185). To say, quite simply, that any codified discourse is open to parody is more methodologically cautious and more true to fact than to assert, as some do, that only mediocre works of art can be parodied (Neumann 1927-8, 439-41). Twentieth-century art forms would not comply with such an observation, even if certain nineteenth-century ones would. It would seem that popular works of art are always parodied, whatever their quality.

Related to the question of what can be parodied is the issue of the scope of parody. Is it a genre, as some have claimed (Dupriez 1977, 332)? It can certainly operate on a wide range of text sizes (Bonfel'd 1977): there have been parodies of the conventions of an entire genre (*pace* Genette's denial (1982, 92); cf. Martin 1972; Shepperson 1967), of the style of a period or movement (Riewald 1966, 126), as well as of a specific artist, where we find parodies of individual works or parts of them (Lelièvre 1954, 66), or of the characteristic aesthetic modes of the entire *œuvre* of that artist. Its physical dimensions can be as vast as Joyce's *Ulysses* or as small as the changing of one letter or word of a text, as in Katherine Fanshawe's oft-quoted parody of Pope's "Here shall the spring its earliest sweets bestow, / Here the first roses of the year shall blow," written on the opening of Regent's Park: "Here shall the spring its earliest coughs bestow, / Here the first noses of the year shall blow" (cited in Postma 1926, 10). Gérard Genette (1982, 40) wants to limit parody to such short texts as poems, proverbs, puns, and titles, but modern parody discounts this limitation, as it does Genette's restricted definition of parody as a minimal transformation of another text (33). While it is obvious that parts of a work may be parodic without the entire text being so labeled (Cabrera Infante's parodies in *Three Trapped Tigers* of the popular song "Guantanamero," of Poe's "The Raven" (the "Poe(t)'s

Ravings"), and of *Alice in Wonderland* (1971, 216-18)), the kind of parody that I shall be dealing with in this study would seem to be an extended form, probably a genre, rather than a technique (cf. Chambers 1974), for it has its own structural identity and its own hermeneutic function.

I would not, however, agree with Riewald in his contention that to be effective a parody must be a "wilful distortion of the entire form *and* spirit of a writer, captured at his most typical moment" (1966, 127). In modern parody, another context can be evoked and then inverted without a step-by-step, pedestrian signaling of the entire form and spirit. Such parody is no less extensive and extended than the one Riewald describes, no matter how economically it is inscribed in the text. In Hemingway's *The Sun also Rises*, for instance, Jake Barnes's name, described as both Flemish and American in the novel (Hemingway 1954, 16), is also, of course, Hebrew. Two readings are therefore simultaneously possible, one in which this modern Jacob struggles in solitude and emerges heroic and affirmative because of his weakness (Schonhorn 1975), and another, ironic one whereby the biblical parody functions as the vehicle of satire. The figure of the fertile and fecund patriarch is now inverted to show us Jake's futile alienation and impotence (Tamke 1967). I think that this kind of signal of a parodic echoing is different in effect from that of the more overt signs employed by more traditional mocking parody, such as the use of a subtitle or a revealing title (Henry Duff Traill's parody of Dante Gabriel Rossetti is entitled "After Dilettante Concetti"; Edward Bradley's of Tennyson is called "In Immemoriam"; William Maginn's of Coleridge is "The Rime of the Auncient Waggonere"). The signals in modern parody are occasionally as overt as this, especially in painting, but the structural and intentional complexity and size of the form I want to examine distinguish it from much of what is generally called parody.

In a similar way, this book also differs from other works on the theory of parody. It is not a history of parody, for the simple reason that many such histories already exist for each of the major national literatures, if not for other art forms. (See, for instance, Courtney 1962, Eidson 1970; Freund 1981; Genette 1982; Hempel 1965; Householder 1944; Kitchin 1931; Koller 1956; Lotman 1973; Macdonald 1960; Markiewicz 1967; Monter 1968; Tuve 1970; Verweyen 1979; Weisstein 1966.) To reattempt this serious and scholarly work would be redundant, not to say foolish. What is important is that all these historians of parody agree that parody prospers in periods of cultural sophistication that enable parodists to rely on the competence of the reader (viewer, listener) of the parody. Another thing that will not be attempted in this study is an anthology or even a survey of parody in this century. Examples will be used from the various art forms as instances of the kinds of works that provoked this reconsideration of the theory of parody. I shall also not attempt a survey of theories of parody. This service has been admirably provided by German theorists like Wolfgang Karrer (1977) and Winfried Freund (1981). What, then, remains to be done?

There are two related contexts into which this book fits. The first is the already mentioned current interest in the modalities of self-reflexivity in modern art, and the second is the emphasis in critical studies today on intertextuality (or transtextuality). The first context is that provided most clearly by Margaret Rose's *Parody//Metafiction* (1979). As her title suggests, she equates parody with self-reference. There are problems with this in her work because parody often becomes synonymous with all textual mirroring or *mise-en-abyme* structures. Parody is certainly one mode of auto-referentiality, but it is by no means the only one. Insistence that it is leads to generalizations that are of dubious validity: "the parodist's mirror is not merely an 'analogue' to truth, but a tool in the supersession of the limitation of art to imitation and representation" (Rose 1979, 66). Rose sees parody as part of a relationship of art to reality (103), rather than one of art to art, with possible implications for the other dimension, as I would argue. Out of this focus on what she calls the sociology of literature comes her confusion of parody with satire. Since her earlier work was on parody in Heine and Marx, it is not surprising that her focus is mostly on the previous century and German Romantic irony, which she calls parody. (Again, sometimes it is, but often it is not.) Rose's Foucaldian reading of the role of parody in literary history is one that makes parody into a mode of discontinuity which rejects earlier kinds of textual reference to other works. Instead, I see parody as operating as a method of inscribing continuity while permitting critical distance. It can, indeed, function as a conservative force in both retaining and mocking other aesthetic forms; but it is also capable of transformative power in creating new syntheses, as the Russan formalists argued. Rose's stress on incongruity, discrepancy, and discontinuity does not account for the forms of twentieth-century parody that we have been examining. Her insistence on the presence of comic effect (without it, any definition, she feels, would not serve "a useful, distinct purpose" as a critical term) is also restrictive. A more neutral definition of repetition with critical difference would allow for the range of intent and effect possible in modern parodic works. Rose is not alone in her limitation of the definition and function of parody. I use her work here only because it is one of the most extended and impressive studies of literary parody as self-reflexivity. But it also reveals the problems that have to be considered if parody is to be given a meaning adequate to the art of today.

The other context in which *A Theory of Parody* situates itself is that of theories of intertextuality. There is no doubt that Gérard Genette's magnificently encyclopedic *Palimpsestes* (1982) is one of the most important works to study transtextuality – the relations (manifest or secret) between texts. His main focus is on "hypertextuality" or the relations (of non-commentary) of one text to an earlier one. Neologisms like "hypertextuality," he argues, have the advantage that everyone at least agrees upon their usage. This is his objection to the term "parody." While I concede the general truth of this objection, my decision to stay with the admittedly abused "parody" is based on more than stubbornness or even resistance to neologism. As will be clear in the next chapter, I think that the etymology of the term offers the best basis for my definition of modern parody. Genette's categories are transhistorical, unlike mine, and therefore he feels that parody in general can only be defined as the minimal transformation of a text. What is good about this definition is its omission of the customary clause about comic or ridiculing effect. This is largely because his is a structural or formal categorization constructed in terms of textual relations alone. When he deals with functions, as he must when he looks at concrete practice, he limits parody to satiric modes (Genette 1982, 34) or to playful *(ludique)* ones, which he then denigrates (453). Genette admits that serious parody could exist, but that then it would not be called parody. In fact, he claims, we have no name for it at all (36). It is clear, I hope, that I disagree.

As a formal analysis of textual interrelations, Genette's work is a superb achievement. Yet, when dividing relations up into imitative ones, the fact that someone imitates and transforms and that someone else perceives and interprets those textual relationships is always in the background of his analysis. Genette acknowledges that his categorizing by function is not a truly pragmatic or hermeneutic procedure. He rejects any definition of transtextuality that depends upon a reader (and implicitly upon an author). It is unacceptable because it is "peu maîtrisable" for a critic who is intent upon categorizing: "elle fait un crédit, et accorde un rôle, pour moi peu supportable, à l'activité herméneutique du lecteur" (16). I quote the original here to give an idea of the strong and personal nature of Genette's rejection of a hermeneutic dimension. He goes on to wish, not surprisingly, for a more conscious and organized pragmatics. While the impulse is understandable in one of France's foremost structural theorists, the reality of the art forms with which I want to deal demands that a pragmatic context be opened up: the author's (or text's) intent, the effect upon the reader, the competence involved in the encoding and the decoding of parody, the contextual elements that mediate or determine the comprehension of parodic modes – all these cannot be ignored, however easier and more "maîtrisable" such a denial would make my project as well. Genette's practice in discussing individual works proves the necessity of this unruly but unignorable dimension: the reader creeps in. Mann's *Doctor Faustus* is said to invite the reader to read Faust beneath Leverkühn; the deciphering of *Oedipus Rex* in Robbe-Grillet's *The Erasers* "doit rester à la charge du lecteur" (354).

My own theoretical perspective here will be dual: both formal and pragmatic. Like Genette, I see parody as a formal or structural relation between two texts. In Bakhtin's terms, it is a form of textual dialogism. In his synthesizing of Bakhtin's diffuse theories, Tzvetan Todorov (1981, 110) noted that parody was a form of passive, divergent, diphonic, represented discourse for Bakhtin. Yet, surely, parody can be considered more active than passive if we move away from the purely structural categories. In other words, even if a definition of modern parody should start with formal analysis, it cannot remain there. In music, for example, a structural, harmonic, rhythmic analysis of the notes themselves cannot account for the difference between Luciano Berio's parodic quotation of Monteverdi in *Recital I (for Cathy)* and Berg's incorporation of Bach's choral "Es ist genug" in his Violin Concerto (Rabinowitz 1981, 194). What is needed is the dual consciousness of the listener of the double-voiced music.

Charles Morris's (1938) early division of semiotics into three parts provides the background for my insistence on a more extended context. In contrast to semantics, which concerns itself with the reference of the sign to its object, and to syntactic studies, which relate signs to each other, pragmatics studies the practical effects of signs. When we speak of parody, we do not just mean two texts that interrelate in a certain way. We also imply an intention to parody another work (or set of conventions) and both a recognition of that intent and an ability to find and interpret the backgrounded text in its relation to the parody. This is where the pragmatic semiotics of a theorist like Umberto Eco offers the tools to go beyond Genette's formalism. Parody would be one of Eco's "inferential walks" that must be taken by the perceiver: "they are not mere whimsical initiatives on the part of the reader, but are elicited by discursive structures and foreseen by the whole textual strategy as indispensable components of the construction" of the work (Eco 1979, 32). On the level of structure, for example, Brecht's *Threepenny Opera* is a parodic reworking and updating of *The Beggar's Opera* (itself a parody of Handel). But would Gay's work necessarily be known to the German audience that Brecht wanted to reach with his political message? Would they, in other words, see it as a doubled operatic parody (as well as a bourgeois satire), even if Brecht (1979, 2, ii, 89-90) and his modern critics did?

My pragmatic perspective would not, however, make parody into a synonym for intertextuality. Today's theories of intertextuality are structural in focus, as we shall see, but depend upon an implied theory of reading or decoding. It is not just a matter of the text's somehow parthenogenetic or magical absorption and transformation of other texts (Jenny 1976, 262; Kristeva 1969, 146). Texts do not generate anything – until they are perceived and interpreted. For instance, without the implied existence of a reader, written texts remain collections of black marks on white pages. Modern art, especially metafiction, has been very aware of this basic fact of aesthetic actualization. The literary theory of Michael Riffaterre reflects this self-consciousness. In his view of intertextuality (1978, 110; 1979a, 9, 90, 97), the experience of literature involves a text, a reader, and his or her reactions, which take the form of systems of words that are grouped associatively in the reader's mind. But in the case of parody those groupings are carefully controlled, like those strategies that Eco sees as governing "inferential walks." What is more, as readers or viewers or listeners who decode parodic structures, we also act as decoders of encoded intent. In other words, parody involves not just a structural *énoncé* but the entire *énonciation* of discourse. This enunciative act includes an addresser of the utterance, a receiver of it, a time and a place, discourses that precede and follow – in short, an entire context (Todorov 1978a, 48). We may know that addresser and its intentions only in the form of inferences that we, as receivers, make from the text, but such inferences are not to be ignored.

The Russian formalists, in all their emphasis and insistence on literariness, never forgot that there was an enunciative context that influenced parody and, indeed, all literature. Èjxenbaum wrote: "The relations between the facts of the literary order and facts extrinsic to it cannot simply be causal relations but can only be relations of correspondence, interaction, dependency, or conditionality" (1978a, 61). Note that he did not deny those contextual relations but only specified the nature of their interplay. Tynjanov (1978a, 72) similarly defined a literary system as a system of functions of the literary order which are in continual interrelations with other orders, such as social conventions. The reception and production, as well as the existence, of parody must be taken into account today. Pragmatics sees language as functional, as being both

a system and a historical product (van Dijk 1977, 167). Morris's relationship between signs and their users is a dynamic communicative
situation involving two agents. In simple direct speech, the speaker would
be the actual agent and the listener would be a possible one. In works
of art, the only actual agents would be the perceivers; the artists would
only be potential in that they and their intentions must be inferred from
the text. The roles of both intent and effectiveness are obviously very
important to any view of language or coded discourse as an act of
communication.

In his analysis of 450 works on parody, Wolfgang Karrer (1977) used
a grid of both formal and pragmatic categories, because he too felt that
the process of communication was central to the understanding of parody.
This is what I shall refer to as the *énonciation* or the contextualized
production and reception of parodic texts. But, unlike Karrer, I shall
not be interested in how the social and psychological interact with the
established intention, attitude, and competence of either actual addresser
or receiver. It is only the encoded intention, as inferred by the receiver
as decoder, that will be dealt with here. There is clearly a new interest
in "contextualism" today, and any theory of modern parody should also
be premised on the belief that "texts can be understood only when set
against the conventional backgrounds from which they emerge; and . . . the
same texts paradoxically contribute to the backgrounds that determine
their meanings" (Schleusener 1980, 669). When that background is
actually grafted onto the text, as in the form of parody, such contextualism cannot be avoided.

Before outlining the chapters to follow, I should like to explain why
there will be no systematic analysis of techniques of parody in this study.
Given the range of intent and effect – far beyond just ridiculing comedy
– that I have claimed for parody today, it would be very difficult to argue
that exaggeration, understatement, or any other comic rhetorical strategy
was a constant (Highet 1962, 69). When critics like Rose (1980), Karrer
(1977), and Freund (1981) base their typologies of parodies on types of
incongruity, they are implicitly accepting a particular theory of laughter
that, in turn, determines which rhetorical devices they allow themselves
to consider (Rose 1980, 15-16). Sander Gilman's (1976) fine study of
German nineteenth-century theories of parody traces the models of the
comic – Hobbesian and Kantian – that lay beneath both the conflict between the theories of Schiller and Goethe and the reconciliation effected
by Schopenhauer, a necessary step which preceded Nietzsche's synthesis
and movement beyond the terms of a debate that is still going on today
in theories of parody based on theories of the comic. In this, Nietzsche's

parodies are very modern in the sense that I am using the term here. The wide scope of parody today probably prevents our establishing even a generalized technique like "accentuation of peculiarities" (Stone 1914, 10). There are as many possible techniques as there are possible kinds of textual interrelationships of repetition with differentiation (Gilman 1974, 2-3; Revzin 1971). We cannot even claim that parody is necessarily reductive (Shlonsky 1966, 797) or even, more simplistically, that it is abbreviating in form. (Some very traditional parodies, like Housman's of Longfellow's "Excelsior," incorporate the original and extend – indeed, in this case, double – its length.)

What we are left with is the need to define both the nature and pragmatic functions of parody as we know it today. Chapter 2 will discuss in more detail the working concept of parody offered in this introduction. The limitations of the standard definitions will be examined, from both a formal and a pragmatic perspective, and the new definition will be used to differentiate parody from other genres that are often confused with it: pastiche, burlesque, travesty, plagiarism, quotation, allusion, and especially satire. It will study the special interaction of irony and parody, since irony is the major rhetorical strategy deployed by the genre. We shall see that structural similarities point to their mutual hermeneutic reinforcement.

This second chapter is important, if only because the shared characteristic of most work done on parody, from a theoretical or practical point of view, is a confusion about the boundaries of the form. Dictionary definitions do not help, for they often define one genre in terms of the other (parody as burlesque, travesty as parody). Highet (1962) wants to make parody a type of satire; Lehmann (1963), on the contrary, sees satire as a dimension of the parodic text. Even those who are careful to separate parody and satire can often not conceive of their interaction as being anything but "accidental" (Dane 1980, 145). Although parody is an "intramural" form with aesthetic norms, and satire's "extramural" norms are social or moral, historically their interaction seems hardly to need documentation. Yet we must be careful to keep them separate, even in more traditional forms. "The Old Man's Comforts" by Southey, with its moral to youth to live moderately, is parodied by Lewis Carroll's "Father William" in such a way that there is both a satire of this specific moral, and a parody of the process of moralizing in poetry. A more modern example would be Woody Allen's parody of *Casablanca* in *Play It Again Sam*. The actual physical incorporation of the earlier film in the opening sequence and the presence of the Rick/Bogart figure point to the parodic inversions. Yet the protagonist is not an antihero; he is a real hero, and his final sacrifice in the name of marriage and friendship is the modern and personal analogue to Rick's more political and public act. What is parodied is Hollywood's aesthetic tradition of allowing only a certain kind of mythologizing in film; what is satirized is our need for such heroicization. The same is true, of course, of *Don Quijote:* the parody of the epic and chivalric romance conventions interacts with the satire against the one who feels that such heroicization in literature is potentially transferable to reality.

Chapter 3 will return to that stubborn retention of the characteristic of ridicule or of the comic in most definitions of parody, a retention that modern parodic practice contests. In its place, I would suggest a range of pragmatic "ethos" (ruling intended effects), from the reverential to the playful to the scornful. The model elaborated here has, I feel, a number of advantages over Morson's (1981) adoption of Bakhtin's evaluative distinction between shallow and deep parody. In addition, the pragmatic role of irony in the production and reception of parody must be taken into account, as must that overlapping of function between parody and satire.

If there exists a relatively wide range of ethos, can we agree with Bakhtin (1968) that there is such a thing as deep or true parody that is a genuinely revolutionary genre? Or must we also account for the reverential and mocking aspects, by both of which parody can be seen as being a conservative force (Barthes 1974; Kristeva 1969; Macdonald 1960)? The novelist John Banville sees his *Nightspawn* as a manifestation of his distrust of the novel form: "I set out to subject the traditional, nineteenth-century concept to as much pressure as I could bring to bear on it, while yet remaining within the rules" (cited in Imhof 1981, 5). Note that he said he wanted to remain within the rules, even as he transgressed them. This is what will be investigated in Chapter 4 as a central paradox of parody: its transgression is always authorized. In imitating, even with critical difference, parody reinforces. Even Max Beerbohm's parodies in *A Christmas Garland* might be seen to suggest less a rejection of the methods of those writers parodied than a situation in which they are still negotiable (Felstiner 1972, 217). Despite Bakhtin's rejection of modern parody, there are close links between what he called carnivalesque parody and the authorized transgression of parodic texts today. In Foucaldian terms, transgression becomes the affirmation of limited being (Foucault 1977, 35). Parody is fundamentally double and divided; its ambivalence stems from the dual drives of conservative and revolutionary forces that are inherent in its nature as authorized transgression.

Chapter 5 examines the pragmatic and formal requirement that, in order for parody to be recognized and interpreted, there must be certain codes shared between encoder and decoder. The most basic of these is that of parody itself (Jenny 1976, 258), for, if the receiver does not recognize that the text is a parody, he or she will neutralize both its pragmatic ethos and its doubled structure. According to Dwight Macdonald: "A peculiar combination of sophistication and provinciality is needed for a good parody, the former for obvious reasons, the latter because the audience must be homogeneous enough to get the point" (1960, 567). The potential for elitism in parody has frequently been pointed out, but little attention has been paid to the didactic value of parody in teaching or co-opting the art of the past by textual incorporation and ironic commentary. Maybe we do need those sleeve notes on modern composers' records in order to understand the music. Maybe Stuart Gilbert's (1930) guide to *Ulysses* is obligatory for many of us. Inferring authorial intent from a text's inscription of it is not always easy, though it need not be impossible. Many cultural codes are shared, even if we, as receivers of texts, have to be reminded of them. The various *Star Wars* films have all been parodies of, among other texts, *The Wizard of Oz*. The very un-Cowardly Lion has been transformed into the Chewbacca, the Wookie; the Tin Man is the futuristic robotic C3P0; the puppy is now R2D2. The munchkins reappear as various helpful small creatures, different in each film. Heavenly pathways replace the yellow-brick road, but the evil witch (here, the Emperor) is still androgynous, dressed in black, and literally cast away at the end of the third movie. Other obvious parodies are also operating: C3P0 and R2D2 are a mechanized Laurel and Hardy; Solo, Luke and Chewy are the new Three Musketeers. There are other more isolated parodies that not all members of the audience might catch: the space fight action, for instance, is directly modeled on the "choreography" of Hollywood World War II movie dogfights, and, in one of the films, Chewbacca picks up C3P0's detached, skull-like head, holds it in one hand, and grunts – but the grunts have the rhythmic syntax of Hamlet's "Alas, poor Yorick! I knew him, Horatio; a fellow of infinite jest, of most excellent fancy." The necessary shared codes in each case are different from the filmic ones of *Oz*, but in all cases the decoder's competence is involved. So too is the inference of intent.

Imitating art more than life, parody self-consciously and self-critically recognizes its own nature. For precisely this reason, it has attracted commentators like David Caute (1972) and Mikhail Bakhtin (1981), for whom ideology and formalism are not mutually exclusive concerns. While it is true that parody invites a more literal and aesthetic interpretation of a text, Chapter 6 will examine how parody is by no means unrelated, as Jonathan Culler, however, insists it is, to what he calls mimesis – that is, to "a serious statement of feelings about real problems or situations" (1975, 153). The mimetic, and ideological status of parody is more subtle than this: both the authority and transgression implied by parody's textual opacity must be taken into account. All parody is overtly hybrid and double-voiced. This is as true of Post-Modern architecture as it is of modernist verse. Paolo Portoghesi's "architecture born of architecture" (1979, 15) is a dialogue with the forms of the past, but a dialogue that recirculates rather than immortalizes. It is never "a turning back to waken the dead, in self-satisfying, narcissistic forms of reflection" (Moschini 1979, 13). Parody is a form of auto-referentiality, but that does not mean that it has no ideological implications.

Obviously, other critics and theoreticians of parody besides myself have noted the existence and significance of parodic forms in the art of the twentieth century. G. D. Kiremidjian writes:

> The widespread presence of parody suggests a greater importance in the very ways in which modern imagination and modern sensibility have been formed, and also suggests the organic function it has had in the development of the primary modes of expression for perhaps the past one hundred years.
>
> (1969, 231)

When a reviewer in *The Times Literary Supplement* can refer to the "fashionable post-modernist principle which decrees that the more parodistic a work of art is, the better" (Morrison 1982, 111), parody may have moved from being a potential paradigm of modern aesthetic form to being a cliché. Parody seems, to many, to have ceased being a way to new forms, as the Russian formalists believed, and to have become – ironically – a model of the prevailing norm. We can think of the reworking of canonized conventions in the music of Ralph Vaughan Williams or Charles Ives, or in the fiction of D. M. Thomas or Robert Nye. Peter Conrad (1980) has argued that the entire work of Salvador Dali can be seen as existing in a parodic relationship with modernism's dissolution of the organic material world – by light fission (impressionism), abstraction (cubism), mechanization (Léger, Picabia), and so on. Dali's famous *Persistence of Memory*, the painting of the dripping, very organic, and unmechanical watches, is certainly a parodic inversion of the conventions of modernism in their horror of the organic. Still others see all modern art, and even all museums (Clair 1974), as the locus of parodic subversion.

As early as 1919, T. S. Eliot argued that all literature possesses "a simultaneous existence and composes a simultaneous order" (1966, 14), and that the poet and critic therefore needed to cultivate their "historical sense." Northrop Frye claimed that he wrote his *Anatomy of Criticism* as an extended annotation to this belief (1970, 18). It was also in 1919 that Viktor Šklovskij made the connection between this view of art and parody: "Not only a parody, but also in general any work of art is created as a parallel and a contradiction to some kind of model" (1973, 53). More recent theorists, such as Antoine Compagnon (1979), have wanted to make the related notion of quotation take on this paradigmatic function; others, like Michael Riffaterre, have offered intertextuality. Still others see parody as the model for all art's relationship with its past and present (Klein 1970, 376) or for the distance that all art has from the object it imitates (Macherey 1978; Weisgerber 1970, 42).

My own aim is more limited. Parody has existed in many, but apparently not all, cultures; its omnipresence today appears to me to demand a reconsideration of both the formal definition and pragmatic functions of parody. It is certainly a mode of self-reflexivity, though not, I think, a true paradigm of fictionality or the fiction-making process (cf. Rose 1979 and Priestman 1980). Parody is a complex genre, in terms of both its form and its ethos. It is one of the ways in which modern artists have managed to come to terms with the weight of the past. The search for novelty in twentieth-century art has often – ironically – been firmly based in the search for a tradition. In Thomas Mann's *Doctor Faustus*, the Devil tells the composer Leverkühn that "bindingly valid conventions" are necessary to guarantee the "freedom of play" (Mann 1948, 241). The master of parodic form replies: "A man could know that and recognize freedom above and beyond all critique. He could heighten the play, by playing with forms out of which, as he well knew, life had disappeared." The Devil's subsequent reply – in its contrast to traditional notions of parody – should serve as a good introduction to the complexity of the genre that today refuses to be limited to ridiculing imitation: "I know, I know. Parody. It might be fun, if it were not so melancholy in its aristocratic nihilism."

2

DEFINING PARODY

Let no one parody a poet unless he loves him.   *Sir Theodore Martin*

A *parody,* a *parody* with a kind of miraculous gift to make it absurder
than it was.   *Ben Jonson*

The German Romantic predecessors of Thomas Mann, self-conscious
about the ontological duality of the work of art, attempted to destroy
what they felt to be artistic illusion. This Romantic irony, of course,
served less to subvert illusion than to create a new one. For their heirs,
modern writers like Mann, this same kind of irony becomes a major
means of creating new levels of illusion by activating that extended but
not always ridiculing type of parody. We have seen that *Doctor Faustus*
is a novel about parody; it is also, like *Felix Krull* and many of Mann's
other novels (Eichner 1952), itself a multiple parody (Heller 1958b), in
the sense of that broader definition just outlined. Irony and parody
become the major means of creating new levels of meaning – and illusion. This type of parody informs both the structure and the thematic
content of Mann's work (Heller 1958a). But, as we have seen, Mann is
not alone in his use of this particular admixture of irony and parody,
and literature does not have a monopoly on self-conscious art today.
It does, however, make its teachings most explicit and therefore articulate,
and it does so in such a way that it provides the clearest examples: there
is less of that need to go to the sleeve notes of records to get the lists
of works parodied, as is the case with much modern music.

Gérard Genette (1982, 235-6) has pointed out the predilection of modern
novelists to turn to earlier forms in their practice of what he chooses
to call "hypertextuality." But it is not just a matter of formal borrowing.

Readers know that much has happened, in literary terms, between the eighteenth century and John Barth's *The Sot-Weed Factor* (1960). The essence of the narrative form which has come to be called metafiction (Scholes 1970) lies in the same acknowledging of the double or even duplicitous nature of the work of art that intrigued the German Romantics: the novel today often still claims to be a genre rooted in the realities of historical time and geographical space, yet narrative is presented as only narrative, as its own reality – that is, as artifice. Often overt narratorial comment or an internal self-reflecting mirror (a *mise-en-abyme*) will signal this dual ontological status to the reader. Or – and this is what is of particular interest in the present context – the pointing to the literariness of the text may be achieved by using parody: in the background will stand another text against which the new creation is implicitly to be both measured and understood. The same is true in the other arts. In the background of Mel Ramos's *Leta and the Pelican* stand not just all those mythological paintings of Leda and the swan, but *Playboy*'s centerfolds (complete with gatefold marks). What is interesting is that, unlike what is more traditionally regarded as parody, the modern form does not always permit one of the texts to fare any better or worse than the other. It is the fact that they *differ* that this parody emphasizes and, indeed, dramatizes.

Irony appears to be the main rhetorical mechanism for activating the reader's awareness of this dramatization. Irony participates in parodic discourse as a strategy, in Kenneth Burke's sense (1967, 1), which allows the decoder to interpret and evaluate. For instance, in a novel which in many ways is a touchstone for this entire re-evaluation of parody, *The French Lieutenant's Woman*, John Fowles juxtaposes the conventions of the Victorian and the modern novel. The theological and cultural assumptions of both ages – as manifest through their literary forms – are ironically compared by the reader through the medium of formal parody. The same signaling of distance and difference can be seen in Iris Murdoch's ironic rehandling of *Hamlet* in *The Black Prince*. In the visual arts, the variety of possible modes is greater than in literature, it seems. For instance, John Clem Clarke poses his friends as Paris, Hermes, and the three goddesses of Rubens's *Judgement of Paris*, and changes the posture to suggest more modern seductive poses. George Segal's plaster sculpture version of Matisse's *Dance* is called *The Dancers*, but his figures, despite the similarity of pose, appear not at all ecstatic; in fact, they seem distinctly self-conscious and ill at ease.

It is the difference between parodic foreground and parodied background that is ironically played upon in works like these. Double-directed irony seems to have been substituted for the traditional mockery or ridicule of the "target" text. In the previous chapter I argued that there are no transhistorical definitions of parody. The vast literature on parody in different ages and places makes clear that its meaning changes. Twentieth-century art teaches that we have come a long way from the earliest sense of parody as a narrative poem of moderate length using epic meter and language but with a trivial subject (Householder 1944, 3). Most theorists of parody go back to the etymological root of the term in the Greek noun *parodia,* meaning "counter-song," and stop there. A closer look at that root offers more information, however. The textual or discursive nature of parody (as opposed to satire) is clear from the *odos* part of the word, meaning song. The prefix *para* has two meanings, only one of which is usually mentioned – that of "counter" or "against." Thus parody becomes an opposition or contrast between texts. This is presumably the formal starting point for the definition's customary pragmatic component of ridicule: one text is set against another with the intent of mocking it or making it ludicrous. The *Oxford English Dictionary* calls parody:

> A composition in prose or verse in which the characteristic turns of thought and phrase in an author or class of authors are imitated in such a way as to make them appear ridiculous, especially by applying them to ludicrously inappropriate subjects; an imitation of a work more or less closely modelled on the original, but so turned as to produce a ridiculous effect.

However, *para* in Greek can also mean "beside," and therefore there is a suggestion of an accord or intimacy instead of a contrast. It is this second, neglected meaning of the prefix that broadens the pragmatic scope of parody in a way most helpful to discussions of modern art forms, as we shall see in the next chapter. But, even in terms of formal structure, the doubleness of the root suggests the need for more neutral terms of discussion. There is nothing in *parodia* that necessitates the inclusion of a concept of ridicule, as there is, for instance, in the joke or *burla* of burlesque. Parody, then, in its ironic "trans-contextualization" and inversion, is repetition with difference. A critical distance is implied between the backgrounded text being parodied and the new incorporating work, a distance usually signaled by irony. But this irony can be playful as well as belittling; it can be critically constructive as well as destructive. The pleasure of parody's irony comes not from humor in particular but from the degree of engagement of the reader in the intertextual "bouncing" (to use E. M. Forster's famous term) between complicity and distance.

It is this same mixture that we find on the level of encoded intent as well in Picasso's many reworkings of Velázquez's *Las Meninas* or in Augustus John's play with El Greco in *Symphonie Espagnole*. In his novella, "The Ebony Tower," John Fowles thematizes this parodic play in terms relevant to all the art forms of our century. The protagonist, a very "modern" artist, regards the very different work of a master parodist:

> As with so much of Breasley's work there was an obvious previous iconography – in this case, Uccello's *Night Hunt* and its spawn down through the centuries; which was in turn a challenged comparison, a deliberate risk...just as the Spanish drawings had defied the great shadow of Goya by accepting its presence, even using and parodying it, so the memory of the Ashmolean Uccello somehow deepened and buttressed the painting before which David sat. It gave an essential tension, in fact: behind the mysteriousness and the ambiguity...behind the modernity of so many of the surface elements there stood both a homage and a kind of thumbed nose to a very old tradition. (Fowles 1974, 18)

It is this combination of respectful homage and ironically thumbed nose that often characterizes the particular kind of parody we shall be considering here.

When Fowles (1969b, 287-8) compared his *The French Lieutenant's Woman* to Thackeray's *Lovel the Widower* with regard to point of view, use of the present tense, and a certain teasing of the reader mixed with ironic self-mockery, it was to remind us that he did not intend to copy, but to recontextualize, to synthesize, to rework conventions – in a respectful manner. This intent is not unique to modern parody, for there is a similar tradition in earlier centuries, even if it does tend to get lost in most critical generalizations. Its most famous articulation is probably J. K. Stephen's "A Parodist's Apology": "If I've dared to laugh at you, Robert Browning, / 'Tis with eyes that with you have often wept: / You have oftener left me smiling or frowning, / Than any beside, one bard except" (cited in Richardson 1935, 9). While modern parodists often add an ironic dimension to this respect, the irony can cut both ways when two texts meet.

As the next chapter will examine in more detail, irony is a so-called sophisticated form of expression. So, too, parody is a sophisticated genre in the demands it makes on its practitioners and its interpreters. The encoder, then the decoder, must effect a structural superimposition of texts that incorporates the old into the new. Parody is a bitextual synthesis (Golopenţia-Eretescu 1969, 171), unlike more monotextual forms like pastiche that stress similarity rather than difference. In some ways, parody might be said to resemble metaphor. Both require that the decoder construct a second meaning through inferences about surface statements and supplement the foreground with acknowledgement and knowledge of a backgrounded context. Rather than argue, as does Wayne Booth (1974, 177), that, although similar in structure to metaphor (and therefore to parody), irony is "subtractive" in terms of strategy in its directing of the decoder away from the surface meaning, I would say that both levels of meaning must coexist structurally in irony, and that this similarity to parody on the formal level is what makes them so compatible.

It should be clear from the discussion that it is very difficult to separate pragmatic strategies from formal structures when talking of either irony or parody: the one entails the other. In other words, a purely formal analysis of parody as text relations (Genette 1982) will not do justice to the complexity of these phenomena; nor will a purely hermeneutic one which, in its most extreme form, views parody as created by "readers and critics, not by the literary texts themselves" (Dane 1980, 145). While the act and form of parody are those of incorporation, its function is one of separation and contrast. Unlike imitation, quotation, or even allusion, parody requires that critical ironic distance. It is true that, if the decoder does not notice, or cannot identify, an intended allusion or quotation, he or she will merely naturalize it, adapting it to the context of the work as a whole. In the more extended form of parody which we have been considering, such naturalization would eliminate a significant part of both the form and content of the text. The structural identity of the text as a parody depends, then, on the coincidence, at the level of strategy, of decoding (recognition and interpretation) and encoding. As we shall see in a later chapter, these are the two parts of the *énonciation* that our post-Romantic formalist age has considered most problematic.

Within a pragmatic frame of reference, however, we can begin to account for the fact that parody involves more than just textual comparison; the entire enunciative context is involved in the production and reception of the kind of parody that uses irony as the major means of accentuating, even establishing, parodic contrast. This does not mean, however, that we can afford to ignore those formal elements in our definitions. Both irony and parody operate on two levels – a primary, surface, or foreground; and a secondary, implied, or backgrounded one. But the latter, in both cases, derives its meaning from the context in which it is found. The final meaning of irony or parody rests on the recognition of the superimposition of these levels. It is this doubleness of *both* form and pragmatic effect or ethos that makes parody an important mode of modern self-reflexivity in literature (for Salman Rushdie, Italo Calvino,

Timothy Findley, and others), music (for Bartók, Stravinsky, Prokofiev, and those contemporary composers we have considered), architecture (Post Modern, in particular), film (for Lucas and Bogdanovich, for instance), and the visual arts (for Francis Bacon, Picasso, and many more).

Many of these artists have openly claimed that the ironic distance afforded by parody has made imitation a means of freedom, even in the sense of exorcizing personal ghosts – or, rather, enlisting them in their own cause. Proust certainly seems to have seen his reworkings of Flaubert as purgative antidotes to the "toxins of admiration" (in Painter 1965, 100). But, for the decoder of parody, this creative function for an individual artist is less important than the realization that, for whatever reason, the artist's parodic incorporation and ironic "trans-contextualization" or inversion has brought about something new in its bitextual synthesis. Perhaps parodists only hurry up what is a natural procedure: the changing of aesthetic forms through time. Out of the union of chivalric romance and a new literary concern for everyday realism came *Don Quijote* and the novel as we know it today. Parodic works like this one – works that actually manage to free themselves from the backgrounded text enough to create a new and autonomous form – suggest that the dialectic synthesis that is parody might be a prototype of the pivotal stage in that gradual process of development of literary forms. In fact, this is the view of parody of the Russian formalists.

Their theory of parody is of interest here because they too saw it as a mode of auto-reflexivity, as a way of pointing to the conventionality they felt was central to the definition of art. Consciousness about form, as achieved by writers like Sterne (and Barth, Fowles, and others today) by its deformation (Šklovskij 1965) through parody, is one possible mode of denuding contrast, of defamiliarizing "trans-contextualization," or of deviation from aesthetic norms established by usage. The implied questioning of these norms also provides the basis for the phenomenon of counter-expectation that allows for the structural and pragmatic activation of parody (Tomachevski 1965, 284) by the decoder. In *Gogol' i Dostoevskij. K teorii parodii*, Tynjanov revealed Dostoevsky's inscribed indebtedness to Gogol, but also his use of parody as a mode of emancipation from him (Erlich 1955, 1965, 93, 194). Parody, therefore, is both a personal act of supersession and an inscription of literary-historical continuity. From this came the formalists' theory of parody's role in the evolution or change of literary forms. Parody was seen as a dialectic substitution of formal elements whose functions have become mechanized or automatic. At this point, the elements are "refunctionalized," to use their term. A new form develops out of the old, without really destroying it; only the function is altered (Èjxenbaum 1965 and 1978b; Tomachevski 1965; Tynjanov 1978a). Parody therefore becomes a constructive principle in literary history (Tynjanov 1978b).

The Russian formalists were not the only ones to stress this historical role of parody. We have already seen Thomas Mann's thematizing of it in his work, and Dürrenmatt wrote of its role in the breaking down of outworn "Ideologie-Konstrukte" (Freund 1981, 7). But much recent theorizing on parody has obviously been influenced by the formalists, either directly or indirectly. Northrop Frye feels that parody is "often a sign that certain vogues in handling conventions are getting worn out" (1970, 103), and Kiremidjian defines parody as "a work which reflects a fundamental aspect of art that is at the same time a symptom of historical processes which invalidate the normal authenticity of primary forms" (1969, 241). Their influence is even seen in Lotman's (1973, 402-3) rejection of a central role for parody in literary evolution. There is little doubt that parody can have a role in change. If a new parodic form does not develop when an old one becomes insufficiently "motivated" (to use the formalists' term) through overuse, that old form might degenerate into pure convention: witness the popular novel, the bestseller of Victorian times or our own. In a more general perspective, however, this view implies a concept of literary evolution as improvement that I find hard to accept. The forms of art *change*, but do they really *evolve* or get better in any way? Again, my definition of parody as imitation with critical difference prevents any endorsement of the ameliorative implications of the formalists' theory, while it obviously allows agreement with the general idea of parody as the inscription of continuity and change.

My attempt to find a more neutral definition that would account for the particular kind of parody displayed by the art forms of this century has an interesting antecedent. In the eighteenth century, when the valuing of wit and the predominance of satire brought parody to the forefront as a major literary mode, one might expect definitions of it to include the element of ridicule that we find even in today's dictionaries. Yet Samuel Johnson defined parody as "a kind of writing, in which the words of an author or his thoughts are taken, and by a slight change adapted to some new purpose." Although it is true that this defines plagiarism as well, it does have the singular merit of not limiting the ethos of parody. Susan Stewart's much more recent definition shares this advantage: parody consists of "substituting elements within a dimension of a given text in such a way that the resulting text stands in an inverse or incongruous relation to the borrowed text" (1978, 1979, 185), although the mention of incongruity suggests an implied theory of laughter that may represent the element of ridicule sneaking in by the back door. I prefer to retain my simple definition. I think it expresses certain common denominators of all theories of parody for all ages, but it is also, for me, a particular necessity for dealing with modern parodic art. By this definition, then, parody is repetition, but repetition that includes difference (Deleuze 1968); it is imitation with critical ironic distance, whose irony can cut both ways. Ironic versions of "trans-contextualization" and inversion are its major formal operatives, and the range of pragmatic ethos is from scornful ridicule to reverential homage.

The danger of such a definition is that it might appear to risk confusing the limits of the genre's boundaries even more than is already the case. The rest of the chapter will be devoted to showing that this is, in fact, not necessarily true. In defining parody in both formal and pragmatic terms, however, it might be argued that I have reduced it to intertextuality. Following Kristeva's (1969, 255) lead, some contemporary theorists have tried to make intertextuality into a purely formal category of textual interaction (Genette 1982, 8; Jenny 1976, 257). It is the supreme value of the work of Michael Riffaterre that it acknowledges the fact that only a reader (or, more generally, a decoder) can activate the intertext (1980a, 626). Riffaterre, like Roland Barthes (1975b, 35-6), defines intertextuality as a modality of perception, an act of decoding texts in the light of other texts. For Barthes, however, the reader is free to associate texts more or less at random, limited only by individual idiosyncrasy and personal culture. Riffaterre, on the other hand, argues that the text in its "structured entirety" (1978, 195n.) demands a more conditioned and therefore more limited reading (1974, 278). Parody would obviously be an even more extreme case of this, because its constraints are deliberate and, indeed, necessary to its comprehension. But, in addition to this extra restricting of the intertextual relationship between decoder and text, parody demands that the semiotic competence and intentionality of an inferred encoder be posited. Therefore, although my theory of parody is intertextual in its inclusion of both the decoder and the text, its enunciative context is even broader: both the encoding and the sharing of codes between producer and receiver are central and will be the subject of Chapter 5.

The framework in which my definition of parody *does* situate itself, unavoidably, is that of other forms of textual imitation and appropriation. The classical and Renaissance belief in the value of imitation as a means of instruction has been passed down through the centuries. Antoine Albalat's *La Formation du style par l'assimilation des auteurs* (1910) is an updated version of those earlier manuals of rhetoric. But imitation in such contexts often meant pastiche or parody. Which? Well, the distinction proves difficult: Proust used both terms for his ironic imitations of Balzac, Flaubert, Michelet, and others. Is Beerbohm's (1921) "The Mote in the Middle Distance" (*A Christmas Garland* (1921)) a parody or a pastiche of the late style of James, with its broken sentences, italics, double negatives, and vague adjectives? Is pastiche more serious and respectful than parody (Idt 1972-3, 134)? Or would that be true only if the concept of parody that was used insisted on ridicule in its description? Since my definition allows for a wide range of ethos, it would not seem possible for me to distinguish parody from pastiche on those grounds. However, it seems to me that parody does seek differentiation in its relationship to its model; pastiche operates more by similarity and correspondence (Freund 1981, 23). In Genette's (1982, 34) terms, parody is transformational in its relationship to other texts; pastiche is imitative.

Although neither parody nor pastiche, as used by someone like Proust, can be considered as trivial game-playing (Amossy and Rosen 1974), there may be a difference in textual localization that makes pastiche seem more superficial. One critic calls it "form-rendering" (Wells 1919, xxi). Pastiche usually has to remain within the same genre as its model, whereas parody allows for adaptation; Georges Fourest's sonnet on Corneille's play *Le Cid* ("Le palais de Gormaz...") would be a parody, rather than a pastiche *à la manière de* Corneille. Pastiche will often be an imitation not of a single text (Albertsen 1971, 5; Deffoux 1932, 6; Hempel 1965, 175) but of the indefinite possibilities of texts. It involves what Daniel Bilous (1982; 1984) calls the interstyle, not the intertext. But, once again, it is similarity rather than difference that characterizes the relationship between the two styles. Parody is to pastiche, perhaps, as rhetorical trope is to cliché. In pastiche and cliché, difference can be said to be reduced to similarity. This is not to say that a parody cannot contain (or use to parodic ends) a pastiche: Joyce's "Oxen of the Sun" episode, with its wide range of virtuoso stylistic imitations, would be a most obvious example (Levin 1941, 105-7).

Both parody and pastiche not only are formal textual imitations but clearly involve the issue of intent. Both are acknowledged borrowings. Herein lies the most obvious distinction between parody and plagiarism. In imprinting upon its own form that of the text it parodies, a parody can ease the decoder's interpretive task. There would be no need in literature, for example, to resort to "stylometry," the statistical analysis of style to determine authorship (Morton 1978). Although there have been many famous cases of forgery in both art and literature (see Farrer 1907; Whitehead 1973), such hoaxes as the Rimbaud "Chasse spirituelle"

(Morrissette 1956) and the *Spectra* collection (Smith 1961) are fundamentally different from parody in their desire to conceal, rather than engage the decoder in the interpretation of their backgrounded texts. The close relationship between pastiche (which aims at similarity) and plagiarism is articulated in a most amusing fashion in Hubert Monteilhet's novel *Mourir à Francfort* (1975). The protagonist, a professor and secret novelist, decides to revive a little-known novel by the Abbé Prévost and publish it under a pseudonym, as he does all his novels. He views his slight reworking of it as a playful revenge on his publisher, as an elegant if unacknowledged pastiche. Others have different names for it, of course. All of this takes place in a Gidean parody of a double-journal novel superimposed on an inverted detective-story plot (the murder takes place only at the very end), whose moral is that the wages of plagiarism is death.

On a somewhat more serious note, the interaction of parody and plagiarism can be seen in the public response to the publication of D. M. Thomas's *The White Hotel* (1981). Although Thomas acknowledged his borrowing from Dina Pronicheva's eyewitness account as the sole survivor of Babi Yar on the copyright page of the novel, his more or less verbatim borrowing launched an intense but perhaps ultimately fruitless debate on plagiarism in the pages of *The Times Literary Supplement* in March and April of 1982. It is interesting that no one, I believe, attacked Thomas for plagiarizing Freud's work, though he produced a fine, if invented, example of a Freudian case history in the same novel. Perhaps the Author's Note about his fictionalizing of what he calls the discoverer of the great modern myth of psychoanalysis had forestalled the critics. Or perhaps serious parody is a different thing altogether. For his case history is not Freud's, even if parts of it quote from *Beyond the Pleasure Principle*, which the fictional Freud, like the real one, was writing at the time of the action of the novel. The reader knows that this text is not Freud's, just as he or she knows that the third part of Rochberg's Third String Quartet is not Beethoven's. It is the knowledge of this difference that, quite simply, separates parody and plagiarism. In his novel *Lanark* (1981), Alasdair Gray spoofs the entire debate by providing the reader with a parodic "Index of Plagiarisms" for the novel. We are informed that there are three kinds of literary theft in the book:

> BLOCK PLAGIARISM, where someone else's work is printed as a distinct typographical unit, IMBEDDED PLAGIARISM, where stolen words are concealed within the body of the narrative, and DIFFUSE PLAGIARISM, where scenery, characters, actions or novel ideas have been stolen without the original words describing them. (485)

To reinforce his mockery, he adds: "To save space these will be referred to hereafter as Blockplag, Implag, and Difplag."

The distinction between parody and plagiarism is necessary only because they have indeed been used as synonyms (Paull 1928, 134), and because the issue of intention (to imitate with critical irony or to imitate with intent to deceive) is one that is both complex and hard to verify. This is why I have limited myself to encoded or inferred intention in discussing parody. Can one tell whether Emerson, Lake, and Palmer intended to borrow (parody) or to steal (plagiarize) Bartók's *Allegro Barbaro* in their *The Barbarian?* The title, I feel, suggests the former, but there are others who disagree (Rabinowitz 1980, 246). It is also the issue of intention that is involved in the confusion of parody with burlesque and travesty. If parody is defined in terms of one ethos – that of ridicule – there is bound to be considerable difficulty in distinguishing from among these forms. The history of the terms suggests that this is indeed the case (Bond 1932, 4; Hempel 1965, 164; Karrer 1977, 70-3). Dictionaries do not help much either: the *Oxford English Dictionary* defines both verbs "to burlesque" and "to travesty" identically: "to turn into ridicule by grotesque parody or imitation." More recent theoreticians' attempts at precision have not been much more helpful, hampered as they frequently are by their limited definitions of parody as ridicule. Dwight Macdonald (1960, 557-8) sees travesty as the most primitive of the forms and parody as the broadest. John Jump makes parody into a kind of "high burlesque of a particular work (or author) achieved by applying the style of that work (or author) to a less worthy subject" (1972, 2). Distinctions between high and low forms suggest the categories of another age, of an aesthetic that is much more rigid than ours would appear to be today in its norms. And distinctions that separate style from subject like this (Bond 1932; Davidson 1966; Freund 1981; Householder 1944) suggest a separation of form and content that is, to many theorists, now considered questionable. Both burlesque and travesty do necessarily involve ridicule, however; parody does not. This difference in *required* ethos is certainly one of the things that distinguish these forms, at least according to what modern art teaches.

It is a difference of intent that also serves to distinguish parody from quotation, probably the most frequently suggested analogue to modern parody. Bakhtin may be responsible for the valorization of this model: when writing of Hellenic literature, he noted that there were varying degrees of assimilation and differentiation in the use of quotations: hidden, overt, half hidden (Bakhtin 1981, 68-9). Although this is true of classical literature in general, it is worth reminding ourselves that the purpose of quoting examples from the works of the greats was to lend their prestige and authority to one's own text. The *Rhetorica ad Herennium*, once attributed to Cicero, is quick to warn, however, that citation is not in itself a mark of cultivation. The ancients can at best act as models. This is not quite the use Bakhtin wanted to make of quotations. In fact, a closer look reveals that he saw parody as citation only in a metaphorical sense. The French translation of the passage about the functioning of parody reads: "C'est le genre lui-même, c'est son style, son langage, qui sont *comme insérés entre des guillemets* qui leur donnent un ton moqueur" (1978, 414; my italics). The English retains the metaphoric sense if not the simile: "The genre itself, the style, the language are all put in cheerfully irreverent quotation marks" (1981, 55). Bakhtin wanted to define parody as a form of indirect discourse, as referring to other forms; hence his idea of its being "as if" in quotation marks.

However, when Margaret Rose defines parody as "the critical quotation of preformed literary language with comic effect" (1979, 59), the metaphor has suddenly become literalized. She has, in fact, inverted Michel Butor's (1967) notion that even the most literal quotation is already a kind of parody because of its "trans-contextualization." But is it legitimate to reverse this and claim that all parody is therefore quotation? I think not, despite the fact that there are convincing arguments being mounted these days for making quotation the model for all writing (Compagnon 1979). "Trans-contextualized" repetition is certainly a feature of parody, but the critical distancing that defines parody is not necessarily implicit in the idea of quotation: to refer to a text as a parody is not the same as to refer to it as a quotation, even if parody has been voided of any defining characteristic suggesting ridicule. Both, however, are forms that "trans-contextualize," and one could argue that any change of context necessitates a difference in interpretation (Èjxenbaum 1978b). In both, therefore, there would be that tension between assimilation and dissimilation that Herman Meyer (1968, 6) saw in the use of quotation in the modern German novel. Similarly, both would allow for a wide range of ethos, from the acknowledging of authority to free play, and both would demand certain shared codes to enable comprehension. Quotation, in other words, while itself fundamentally different from parody in some ways, is also structurally and pragmatically close enough that what in fact happens is that quotation becomes a form of parody, especially in modern music and art.

I do not agree with Stefan Morawski that "even the most consummate and versatile connoisseur of the arts would have to rack his memory much harder to recall an example of quotation in painting, theatre or film, than in the case of literature" (1970, 701). And no one who had

seen Thomas Vreeland's quoting of both the Campanile of the Cathedral
in Sienna and Adolf Loos's design for the Josephine Baker House in Paris
in his own World Savings and Loan Association building in Santa Aña,
California, could say that architecture is the art the "least amenable to
quotation" (Morawski 1970, 702). What about Michael Graves's quotation of the broken symmetries and the landscape/building interrelations
of Raphael's sixteenth-century Villa Madama in his 1977 Placek House?

    In the visual arts, semioticians like René Payant (1979, 5) are tempted
to postulate that all paintings quote other paintings. This argument would
be not unlike the Russian formalist insistence on the conventionality of
literature. Both are reactions to a realist aesthetic that values the represen-
tational in art. Many of these citational paintings are, as we have seen,
parodic. The same is true in music's use of quoting in order to effect
contrast. For critics hampered by a ridicule-laden definition of parody,
such quotation is often not considered at all parodic (Gruber 1977; Kneif
1973). Nevertheless there is a general agreement that quotation has
become of central importance to modern music (Kuhn 1972; Siegmund-
Schultze 1977; Sonntag 1977). George Rochberg has traced his development out of serialism and his discovery of the musical traditions of the
past in terms that show the difference between simple and parodic quotation. In the sleeve notes to his String Quartet No. 3 (Nonesuch H-71283),
he talks of his arriving at the conviction that the past should be a "living
present" for composers. He first began by quoting parts of tonal music
in the form of assemblages or collages in his Contra Mortem et Tempus.
But soon commentary was implied in his act of quoting (Nach Bach),
and in the Third String Quartet the parodic synthesis of the new atonality
and the old tonal conventions (nineteenth-century melodic-harmonic
language in general, and the styles of Beethoven and Mahler in particular)
was possible. Similarly Luciano Berio's Sinfonia "trans-contextualizes"
fragmented quotations of Bach, Schoenberg, Debussy, Ravel, Strauss,
Brahms, Berlioz, and others, within the context of the rhythmic impulses
of the third movement of Mahler's Second Symphony. On the record
sleeve (CBC Classics 61079) Berio tells us: "The Mahler movement is
treated like a container within whose framework a large number of
references are proliferated, interrelated and integrated into the flowing
structure of the original work itself." This is what the formalists called
"refunctioning" or parody, although it does involve "trans-contextualizing"
quotation.

    Parody has a stronger bitextual determination than does simple quota-
tion or even allusion: it partakes of both the code of a particular text
parodied, and also of the parodic generic code in general (Jenny 1976,

258). I include allusion here because it too has been defined in ways that have led to confusion with parody. Allusion is "a device for the simultaneous activation of two texts" (Ben-Porat 1976, 107), but it does so mainly through correspondence – not difference, as is the case with parody. However, ironic allusion would be closer to parody, although allusion in general remains a less constricted or "predetermined" form than parody (Perri 1978, 299), which must signal difference in some way. Parody is also often a more extended form of transtextual reference today.

Parody, then, is related to burlesque, travesty, pastiche, plagiarism, quotation, and allusion, but remains distinct from them. It shares with them a restriction of focus: its repetition is always of another discursive text. The ethos of that act of repetition can vary, but its "target" is always intramural in this sense. How, then, does parody come to be confused with satire, which is extramural (social, moral) in its ameliorative aim to hold up to ridicule the vices and follies of mankind, with an eye to their correction? For the confusion certainly does exist. Parody has been implicitly or explicitly called a form of satire by many theorists (Blackmur 1964; Booth 1974; Feinberg 1967; Macdonald 1960; Paulson 1967; Rose 1979; Stone 1914). For some, this is a way of not limiting parody to an aesthetic context, of opening it up to social and moral dimensions (see Karrer 1977, 29-31). While I sympathize with the attempt, two subsequent chapters (4 and 6) will address the complexity of this issue. Just calling parody satire seems a little too simple as an instant way to give parody a social function.

The grounds upon which other theorists do separate the two genres are sometimes debatable. Winfried Freund (1981, 20) claims that satire aims at the restoration of positive values, while parody can only operate negatively. Since her focus is largely on German nineteenth-century literature, parody is said to lack important metaphysical and moral dimensions that satire can demonstrate. But I would argue that the difference between the two forms lies not so much in their perspective on human behavior, as she believes, but in what is being made into a "target." In other words, parody is not extramural in its aim; satire is. Both Northrop Frye (1970, 233-4, 322) and Tuvia Shlonsky (1966, 798) have argued this clearly and convincingly in the face of remarks such as "No aspect of society has been safe from the parodist's mocking attention" (Feinberg 1967, 188). Yet the obvious reason for the confusion of parody and satire, despite this major difference between them, is the fact that the two genres are often used together. Satire frequently uses parodic art forms for either expository or aggressive purposes (Paulson 1967, 5-6), when it desires textual differentiation as its vehicle. Both satire and parody imply critical distancing and therefore value judgments, but satire generally uses that distance to make a negative statement about that which is satirized – "to distort, to belittle, to wound" (Highet 1962, 69). In modern parody, however, we have found that no such negative judgment is necessarily suggested in the ironic contrasting of texts. Parodic art both deviates from an aesthetic norm and includes that norm within itself as backgrounded material. Any real attack would be self-destructive.

The interaction of parody and satire in modern art is pervasive, despite the view of one commentator who has decided that satire is now a minor and outdated form (Wilde 1981, 28). (What do we do with Coover, Pynchon, Rushdie and a spate of other contemporary novelists?) The increased cultural homogeneity in the "global village" has increased the range of parodic forms available for use. In earlier centuries, the Bible and the classics were the major backgrounded texts for the educated class; popular songs provided the vehicle for others. While this is a general rule, there are, of course, always exceptions. Rochester ironically inverted the conventions of religious poetry to cynical and sexual ends in his parodies (Treglown 1973), thereby reversing the Lutheran practice of spiritualizing the secular (Grout 1980). Epic traditions, however, provided the ground for many parodies in the eighteenth century, parodies that are very close to some kinds of modern satiric forms of parody. The mock epic did not mock the epic: it satirized the pretensions of the contemporary as set against the ideal norms implied by the parodied text or set of conventions. Its historic antecedent was probably the *silli* or Homeric parodies, which satirized certain people or ways of life without in any way mocking Homer's work (Householder 1944, 3). There are still other, later examples of the same kind of use of parody and satire as we find in today's art forms. For example, the predecessor of much recent feminist parodic satire is to be found in Jane Austen's fiction. In *Love and Friendship*, Austen parodies the popular romance fiction of her day and, through it, satirizes the traditional view of woman's role as the lover of men. Laura and Sophia live out pre-patterned literary plots and are discredited by Austen's parody of Richardson's literary "heroinization" and its presentation of female passivity. As Susan Gubar has shown, "in her parodies of Fanny Burney and Sir Samuel Egerton Brydges in *Pride and Prejudice*, Austen dramatizes [and satirizes] how damaging it has been for women to inhabit a culture created by and for men" (Gilbert and Gubar 1979, 120). Along with Mary Shelley, Emily and Charlotte Brontë, and other women writers, Austen used parody as the disarming but effective literary vehicle for social satire.

I do not mean to suggest, then, that only modern parody plays with this particular conjunction with the satiric. Most of eighteenth-century literature in England did so too. And Gilbert and Sullivan certainly made almost formulaic use of it: *Iolanthe* parodied the fairy-tale form in order to satirize the peerage. *Princess Ida* was a respectful inversion of Tennyson's *Princess* that served as the vehicle for a satire of women's rights. More within our period of interest, Apollinaire used formal parody to satirize Verlaine's causeless spiritual pain in terms of actual physical discomfort. Rimbaud's "Il pleut doucement sur la ville" forms the epigraph to Verlaine's poem, which begins:

> Il pleure dans mon cœur
> Comme il pleut sur la ville.
> Quelle est cette langueur
> Qui pénètre mon cœur?

Apollinaire's parody reads:

> Il flotte dans mes bottes
> Comme il pleut sur la ville.
> Au diable cette flotte
> Que pénètre mes bottes!

Neither the parody nor the satire is very subtle in this more traditional kind of parody.

In the more extended version that we have been examining, the interaction with satire is more complex. When Joyce's *Ulysses* turns to Homer's *Odyssey*, and Eliot's *The Waste Land* invokes an even more vast tradition, from Virgil through Dante and on to the symbolists and beyond, what is at issue is more than an allusive echoing either of one text or of the cultural patrimony. The discursive practices active at a particular time and in a particular place are involved (Gomez-Moriana 1980-1, 18). The interdiscursive *énonciation*, as well as the intertextual *énoncé*, is implicated. The *Don Quijote* written by that seventeenth-century Spaniard called Cervantes would be different, Borges (1962, 1964, 42-3) has suggested, from the *Quijote* written by a modern French symbolist – let's call him Pierre Menard – even if they are verbally identical texts. Menard's text would be richer because of what has now become deliberate anachronism (and "brazenly pragmatic" historicism). Knowing that Menard would be the contemporary of William James, Borges's narrator can reread the *Quijote* in the light of this philosophical, social, and cultural (as well as literary) "trans-contextualization." This parodic use of literature to help in the ironic judgment of society is not new to our century: Eliot's predecessor in facing the decline of his community and his age through satiric parody is probably Juvenal (Lelièvre 1958). We shall see in the next chapter the role of irony in the seemingly strong compatibility between parody and satire.

For many, the 1960s marked a new golden age of satire (Dooley 1971), but it was a satire that relied very much on parody and therefore shared its variable ethos. In the work of writers like Pynchon and artists like Robert Colescott, there is less of a sense of aiming at what Swift called "no defect / But what all mortals may correct." The black humor (as it was labeled) of these years has begun to change our concept of satire, just as respectful parody has changed our notion of parody. But that is probably the subject of another book. Nevertheless, the interaction of the two genres remains a constant. Much female writing today, aiming as it does to be both revisionary and revolutionary, is "parodic, duplicitous, extraordinarily sophisticated" (Gilbert and Gubar 1979, 80). Short fiction by writers like Barthelme has proved as provocative as longer works because of its economical use of suggestive parody. Max Apple's "The Oranging of America" (1976, 3-19) uses a parody of, obviously, *The Greening of America* to satirize the acquisitive American ethic epitomized by Howard Johnson and his orange-roofed hotels.

Musical satiric parody also has an honorable history. Mozart's *A Musical Joke* parodies certain modish musical conventions (unnecessary repetition of banalities, incorrect modulation, disjointed melodic ideas) as a vehicle for the satire of inept amateur composing and performing – it is also known as the *Village Musician's Sextet*. In a manner which suggests almost a parody of Mozart, the second movement of Charles Ives's Fourth Symphony parodies other pieces of music and at the same time imitates the playing of incompetent performers. In his *The Fourth of July*, the fictional amateur band performance is meant, I suppose, to take an American listener back to the innocence of childhood and fourth of July picnics. There is an interesting tension set up between this nostalgic recall and the realization that this is something different: the technical errors of that band serve as parodic reminders of difference that function satirically to make the listener consider his or her present state of lost innocence.

In the visual arts, there is a wide range of satiric uses of parodic forms. Ad Reinhardt's overt satires of the art scene of New York in the forties and fifties took the form of comic-style illustration/collage pieces, in order to parody those didactic attempts to comprehend the complexity of developments in art by simplistic textbook diagrams. *How to Look at Modern Art in America* is a parody of those synoptic tables of the modernist movements which were used to teach modern art in universities. It is also a satire of the contemporary art scene, through where he placed which artists on the diagram tree (Hess 1974). Although Magritte (1979) himself denied any symbolic or satiric intent in his coffin parodies of David and Manet, most viewers find it hard not to read in the formal parody an ideological comment on a dead aristocratic or bourgeois culture.

Similar satiric intent seems clearer, perhaps, in the work of Masami Teraoka, especially in his parodies of Hokusai's *Thirty-Six Views of Mount Fuji*. One of these, for instance, *New Views of Mount Fuji: Sinking Pleasure Boat*, maintains the Edo costumes for each figure, but one of them has a camera hanging from his neck, and another, a geisha, tries to take a photograph with her tripod – on the sinking ship. Nearby, a samurai reaches for his golf clubs. The traditional ideograms remain, but here they evidently mean things like "Golf Craze." Perhaps the most amusing of these works is *Thirty-One Flavors Invading Japan: French Vanilla*, with its parody of the Japanese erotic print and its satire of the Americanization of Japan (see Lipman and Marshall 1978, 94-5). A similar ironic juxtaposition of erotic traditions is revealed in the work of Mel Ramos. His *Velázquez Version* is a parody of the master's *Venus and Cupid*, but through a second level of parody (of *Playboy* pinups) the narcissism of modern woman is satirized. Perhaps Ramos is also suggesting, by the parodic juxtaposition, that what we find erotic today may, indeed, not have changed. He reworks Manet's *Olympia* and Ingres's *La Grande Odalisque* in much the same way. Andy Warhol goes one better than Duchamp and his Dadaist *L.H.O.O.Q.* with its moustached *Mona Lisa* when he reproduces the Renaissance masterpiece in silkscreen, repeated thirty times. The pop ironic commentary is clear in his title – *Thirty are Better than One* – implying a satire of a consumer society that loves quantity more than quality and therefore can use a popular icon of highbrow art as a mass-produced product. It is also a society, of course, that is willing to pay highbrow prices for Warhol's parodic satire; the market has an infinite capacity to co-opt.

Another example of the interaction of parody and satire is Robert Rauschenberg's *Retroactive I*. In the right corner of this work is a silk-screen enlargement of a Gjon Mili photograph from *Life* magazine. With the help of a stroboscopic flash, it comes strongly to resemble Duchamp's *Nude Descending a Staircase* (which, ironically, was itself based on Marey's photos of a moving body). But, in the context of the work, it ends up looking like a Masaccio Adam and Eve being expelled from Eden. The determining context is that of a photograph of John F. Kennedy (already a godlike cult figure when the work was executed in 1964), who becomes a vengeful God-figure with finger pointed.

5 Mel Ramos, *Plenti-Grand Odalisque*, 1973

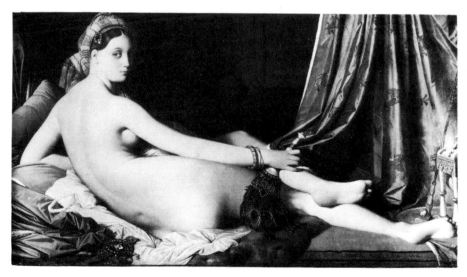

6 J.A.D. Ingres, *La Grande Odalisque*

More popular art forms such as comic strips and television series have also been analyzed to reveal the close interaction of parodic forms and satiric intent. The work of Ziva Ben-Porat (1979) is remarkable among studies of both genres in its lucid study of the conventional nature of both the social referent of the satire and the parodic code used to communicate it. The long definitions of both are worth citing for their precision in making the distinction between the two forms. Parody is defined in basically semiotic terms as an

> alleged representation, usually comic, of a literary text or other artistic object – i.e. a representation of a "modelled reality," which is itself already a particular representation of an original "reality." The parodic representations expose the model's conventions and lay bare its devices through the coexistence of the two codes in the same message. (1979, 247)

Satire, in contrast, is a

> critical representation, always comic and often caricatural, of "non-modelled reality," i.e. of the real objects (their reality may be mythical or hypothetical) which the receiver reconstructs as the referents of the message. The satirized original "reality" may include mores, attitudes, types, social structures, prejudices, and the like. (1979, 247-8)

Ben-Porat's analysis of the interaction of parody and satire in the MAD television series is complex enough not to be reproducible in this context. It is, however, necessary reading for anyone interested in this topic.

There is yet another reason for the confusion between parody and satire in theory and criticism. Parody is not just to be considered as a formal entity, a structure of assimilation or appropriation of other texts. In this confusion, it is not just the intricate textual interaction of parody and satire that is at fault; nor is the ignoring of the difference in the kind of "target" (intra- versus extramural) to blame all the time. The next chapter will address the role of irony in this common mixing of genres, for it is on the pragmatic, as much as the formal, level that parody today differentiates itself, not only from satire, but from those traditional definitions that demand the inclusion of the intent to ridicule.

3

THE PRAGMATIC RANGE
OF PARODY

Every intelligent painter carries the whole culture of modern painting
in his head. It is his real subject, of which everything he paints is
both an homage and a critique.   *Robert Motherwell*

Most studies of parody argue that it is a more restricted form, in pragmatic
terms, than allusion or quotation. In other words, there are many more
possible reasons for alluding or quoting than for parodying. One might
want to circumvent criticism, to hint without directly stating; one might
choose to parade one's knowledge or to use the texts of others for
authoritative support; one might just want to save time (Ben-Porat 1976,
108). Modern parody, however, teaches us that it has many more uses
than traditional definitions of the genre are willing to consider. Nevertheless, many still feel that parody that does anything short of ridiculing its "target" is false parody. One logical conclusion of this sort of
reasoning is that mock epics that do not discredit the epic cannot be so
labeled (Morson 1981, 117). To argue this, of course, is to go against
the entire tradition of the term's usage. I would like to argue that the
same is true of parody in general, despite the long tradition – dating back
to Quintilian (1922, 395), at least – that demands that parody be considered pejorative in intent and ridiculing in its ethos or intended response.
The traditional range allowed seems to be "amusement, derision, and
sometimes scorn" (Highet 1962, 69). Most theorists implicitly agree with
Gary Saul Morson's (1981, 110, 113, 142) view that a parody is intended
to have higher semantic authority than its original and that the decoder
is always sure of which voice he or she is expected to agree with. While
the latter might be true, we have seen that the "target" of parody is not
always the parodied text at all, especially in twentieth-century art forms.

Theodor Verweyen (1979) has separated theories of parody into two categories: those that define it in terms of its comic nature and those that prefer to stress its critical function. What is common to both views, however, is the concept of ridicule. As a subgenre of the comic, parody makes its model ludicrous: this is one tradition. But even as a "department of pure criticism" (Owen Seaman, cited in Kitchin 1931, xix) parody exercises a conservative function, and does so through ridicule, once again. The majority of theorists want to include humor or derision in the very definition of parody (see, for example, Dane 1980; Eidson 1970; Falk 1955; Macdonald 1960; Postma 1926; Stone 1914). This is probably why Max Beerbohm thought parody the specialty of youth rather than mature wisdom (1970, 66).

For others, however, parody is a form of serious art criticism, though its bite is still achieved through ridicule. Admittedly, as a form of criticism, parody has the advantage of being both a re-creation and a creation, making criticism into a kind of active exploration of form. Unlike most criticism, parody is more synthetic than analytic in its economical "trans-contextualizing" of backgrounded material (Riewald 1966, 130). Among those who argue for this function of parody (see Davis 1951; Leacock 1937; Lelièvre 1958; Litz 1965), W. H. Auden perhaps articulated it most memorably. In his "daydream College for Bards" the library would contain no works of literary criticism and "the only critical exercise required of students would be the writing of parodies" (1968, 77). This more serious function of parody has the potential to allow for a wider pragmatic range besides ridicule, yet few choose to extend it in that direction; "critical ridicule" (Householder 1944, 3) remains the most commonly cited purpose of parody.

There have, however, been important oppositions to this limitation of the parodic ethos to one of mockery. Fred Householder (1944, 8) has pointed out that, in classical uses of the word parody, humor and ridicule were not considered part of its meaning; in fact, another word was added when ridicule was intended. In examining the *OED* history of the usage of the word parody in English from 1696 on, Howard Weinbrot (1964, 131) argued that ridicule or burlesque were certainly not the only meanings of the term, especially in the eighteenth-century mock epic, as we too have seen. Yet that century did mark both a valuing of wit and an almost paradigmatic mixing of parody and satire, one that tended to dominate in subsequent attempts to develop a theory of parody; from then on, parody had to be funny and pejorative, as the Abbé de Sallier decreed in 1733. But, if we no longer accept the limitation of the form of parody to a verse composition of a certain kind, why should we accept an outdated limitation of ethos? Within a pragmatic perspective too, there again appears to be no transhistoric definition of parody: nothing is perhaps more culture-dependent than ethos. Why must Sallier's model (which presents the attitude of the parodist to the "target" as one of aggression and ridiculing criticism) necessarily still be relevant today – especially since modern parodic texts from Eliot to Warhol suggest the contrary? Yet, as Wolfgang Karrer (1977, 27) has documented so extensively, most work on parody today still accepts this limitation.

There are a few exceptions to this finding. One critic makes a useful distinction between parodies that use the parodied text as a target and those that use it as a weapon (Yunck 1963). The latter is closer to the truth of modern, extended, ironic parody, while the former is what has more traditionally been considered as parody. Another similar distinction is Markiewicz's (1967, 1271) differentiation between parody "sensu largo," which is imitative recasting, and parody "sensu stricto," which ridicules its model. But both depend, once again, upon the *comic,* instead of upon, as I prefer, the *ironic.* The marking of difference through irony is one way of dealing with what I call the range of parodic ethos, or what others have called its ambivalence (Allemann 1956, 24; Rotermund 1963, 27).

At the end of Chapter 2 I suggested that one of the reasons for the confusion in terminology between satire and parody lay in their common use of irony as a rhetorical strategy. Critics have helped confuse us by announcing that "satire must parody man" (Morton 1971, 35) and that the "hidden irony and satire against the parodied text" is a necessary part of the parodic effect of a work (Rose 1979, 27). As the last quotation suggests, irony does seem to play its role in this taxonomic muddle. As a trope, irony is central to the functioning of both parody and satire, but not necessarily in the same way. The important difference stems from the fact that irony has both a semantic and a pragmatic specificity (Kerbrat-Orecchioni 1980). Therefore, as we found with parody, irony must be examined from a pragmatic perspective as well as from the usual formal (antiphrastic) one. A pragmatic approach that concentrates on the practical effects of signs is particularly relevant to the study of the interaction of verbal irony with parody and satire, because what is required in such a study is an account of the conditions and characteristics of the utilization of the particular system of communication which irony establishes within each genre. In both, the presence of the trope underlines the necessary postulating of both inferred encoded intent and decoder recognition in order for the parody or satire even to exist as such.

There is little disagreement among critics that the interpretation of irony does involve going beyond the text itself (the text as semantic or syntactic entity) to decoding the ironic intent of the encoding agent. Recent work in pragmatics (Warning 1979; Wunderlich 1971) has attempted to define the act of language as a "situated" one, moving beyond Jakobson's (1960) more static model into a wider frame of reference. This kind of "situating" is of obvious interest to a discussion of the contextual usage of irony in parody. Because verbal irony is more than a semantic phenomenon, its pragmatic value is of equal importance and ought to be incorporated as an autonomous ingredient, not just in definitions, but in analyses involving the trope. Catherine Kerbrat-Orecchioni's recent (1980) insistence on this point is of particular interest in the light of her own earlier work (1976), which shared the traditional semantic limitation of irony to antiphrasis, to the opposition between an intended and a stated meaning or, simply, to a marking of contrast (Booth 1974, 10; Muecke 1969, 15). But this semantic contrast between what is stated and what is meant is not the only function of irony. Its other major role – on a pragmatic level – is often treated as if it were too obvious to warrant discussion: irony judges. Yet in this lack of differentiation between the two functions appears to me to lie another key to the taxonomic confusion between parody and satire.

The pragmatic function of irony, then, is one of signaling evaluation, most frequently of a pejorative nature. Its mockery can, but need not, take the usual form of laudatory expressions employed to imply a negative judgment; on a semantic level, this involves the deployment of manifest praise to hide latent mocking blame. Both of these functions – semantic inversion and pragmatic evaluation – are implied in the Greek root, *eironeia*, which suggests dissimulation and interrogation: there is both a division or contrast of meanings, and also a questioning, a judging. Irony functions, therefore, as both antiphrasis and as an evaluative strategy that implies an attitude of the encoding agent towards the text itself, an attitude which, in turn, allows and demands the decoder's interpretation and evaluation. Like parody, then, irony too is one of Eco's "inferential walks" (1979, 32), a controlled interpretive act elicited by the text. Both, therefore, must be dealt with both pragmatically and formally.

In Chapters 1 and 2 a parodic text was defined as a formal synthesis, an incorporation of a backgrounded text into itself. But the textual doubling of parody (unlike pastiche, allusion, quotation, and so on) functions to mark difference. From the double etymology of the prefix *para*, I argued that on a pragmatic level parody was not limited to producing a ridiculous effect (*para* as "counter" or "against"), but that the equally strong suggestion of complicity and accord (*para* as "beside") allowed

for an opening up of the range of parody. This same distinction between
prefix meanings has been used to argue for the existence of both comic
and serious types of parody (Freund 1981, 1-2), but I want to go beyond
this to use it to differentiate the ethos of parody from that of satire, by
examining their common use of irony as a rhetorical strategy. Although
parody is by no means always satirical (Clark and Motto 1973, 44;
Riewald 1966, 128-9), satire frequently uses parody as a vehicle for ridiculing the vices or follies of humanity, with an eye to their correction. This
very definition orients satire toward a negative evaluation and a corrective
intent. Modern parody, on the other hand, rarely has such an evaluative
or intentional limitation. The work of Sylvia Plath has been seen as a
feminist reworking (or parody) of the models of male modernism which
she inherited. Her competitive spirit could drive her to oppose that
heritage, but she could also draw upon it for strength (Gilbert 1983).
The other major difference between the two genres, of course, is that
of the nature – intra- or extramural – of their "targets."

Let us return now to the two functions of irony: the semantic, contrasting one and the pragmatic, evaluative one. On the semantic level,
irony can be defined as a marking of difference in meaning or, simply,
as antiphrasis. As such, paradoxically, it is brought about, in structural
terms, by the superimposition of semantic contexts (what is stated / what
is intended). There is one signifier and two signifieds, in other words.
Given the formal structure of parody, as described in the previous chapter,
irony can be seen to operate on a microcosmic (semantic) level in the
same way that parody does on a macrocosmic (textual) level, because
parody too is a marking of difference, also by means of superimposition
(this time, of textual rather than of semantic contexts). Both trope and
genre, therefore, combine difference and synthesis, otherness and incorporation. Because of this structural similarity, I should like to argue,
parody can use irony easily and naturally as a preferred, even privileged,
rhetorical mechanism. Irony's patent refusal of semantic univocality
matches parody's refusal of structural unitextuality.

The second, evaluative, function of verbal irony has always been
assumed but rarely discussed. Perhaps the difficulty in localizing irony
textually has made theorists shy away from coming to terms with this
other, but very important, function of irony – its pragmatic function.
Most of them agree that the degree of ironic effect in a text is inversely
proportionate to the number of overt signals needed to achieve that effect
(Alleman 1978, 393; Almansi 1978, 422; Kerbrat-Orecchioni 1977, 139).
But signals must perforce exist within the text in order to allow the decoder
to infer the evaluative intent of the encoder. And irony is usually at

someone's or something's expense. It would therefore be in this pragmatic function, and not in the semantic one, that would lie the ready adaptability of mocking irony to the genre of satire.

In other words, in these two different, though obviously complementary, functions of the rhetorical trope of irony might lie that other key to the terminological confusion between parody and satire. Since both utilize irony, though by means of different affinities (one structural, the other pragmatic), they are often confused one with the other. This makes irony of crucial importance in defining and distinguishing between the two genres. But we must go beyond pointing out the formal parallels between irony and parody if we are to understand the complexity of the implications of this generic confusion: we must consider the pragmatics, the practical effects of that encoded, then decoded, message which is to be labeled as parodic.

I have been arguing that we must consider the entire act of the *énonciation*, the contextualized production and reception of texts, if we are to understand what constitutes parody. Therefore we must move beyond those text/reader models of intertextuality to include encoded and then inferred intentionality and semiotic competence. In this same direction, we must also try to expand the receiver-oriented view of parodic communicative interaction best represented by the work of Theodor Verweyen (1973, 1977). I have been using the term "ethos" much in the way defined by the Groupe *MU* (1970, 147), but with an increased emphasis on the encoding process. By ethos I mean the ruling intended response achieved by a literary text. The intention is inferred by the decoder from the text itself. In some ways, then, the ethos is the overlap between the encoded effect (as desired and intended by the producer of the text) and the decoded effect (as achieved by the decoder). Obviously, my use of the term ethos is not like Aristotle's, but it is closely related to his concept of *pathos*, that emotion with which the encoding speaker seeks to invest the decoding listener. An ethos, then, is an inferred intended reaction motivated by the text. If we were to posit an ethos for parody and satire, we would have to include that of irony as well. A simple visualization of the resulting interrelations might look something like Figure 1.

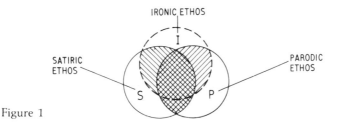

Figure 1

Although this very simple model has the disadvantage of appearing on paper to be as static as Jakobson's (1960), it is meant to be seen as taking the form of three overlapping *and constantly shifting* circles, the proportions of mutual inclusion varying with each particular text being considered. For clarity of analysis, however, each ethos should be discussed in its hypothetically isolated state, before examining their overlappings. The simplicity of this diagram will turn out to be illusory, once we add the dynamic triple interrelationships.

Verbal (not situational) irony is represented in Figure 1 as a broken-line circle in order to remind us that it is a different entity from the others: it is a trope and not a genre. But it too does have an ethos. The generally accepted ethos of irony is a mocking one (Groupe *MU* 1978, 427). In this sense it is "marked" – in the linguistic meaning of the term – as being coded in a definite way: here, pejoratively. Without this mocking ethos, irony would cease to exist, because the pragmatic context (encoded and decoded) is what determines the perception of distance or contrast between semantic contexts. This ethos, however, contains within itself a range of degree from the lighthearted snicker to the cumulative ironic bitterness of Mark Antony's repeated "Brutus is an honourable man" refrain in *Julius Caesar*.

Satire, like irony, possesses a marked ethos, one that is even mc re pejoratively or negatively coded (Morier 1961, 217). This can be called a scornful or disdainful ethos. It is that kind of encoded anger, communicated to the decoder through invective, that led Max Eastman to describe the range of satire as "degrees of biting" (1936, 236). Satire should not be confused with simple invective, however, for the corrective aim of satire's scornful ridicule is central to its identity. While satire can be destructive (Valle-Killeen 1980, 15), there is also an implied idealism, for it is often "unabashedly didactic and seriously committed to a hope in its own power to effect change" (Bloom and Bloom 1979, 16). There is, nevertheless, an aggressive side to satire's ethos, as Freud and Ernst Kris (1964) noted. When we come to discuss the overlapping of satire with irony, we shall see that it would be at the end of the ironic scale of ethos where a contemptuous bitter laugh is produced that satire weds irony most fiercely.

Traditionally, parody too has been considered as having a negatively marked ethos: ridicule. In *Jokes and their Relation to the Unconscious*, Freud (1953-74, vol. VIII) reduced parody to "comic nonsense" (176), but then focused on both its aggressive and its defensive intent (201). The example of Beerbohm's ironic attack on George Moore's reliance on Pater in the Dickens section of *A Christmas Garland* (1921, 179-85) is an example of the kind of parody Freud might have had in mind. Here Beerbohm "has at" the digressions, vagueness, love of trivia, and errors of Moore's essays on Balzac and French impressionism by making Tintoretto Flemish, Palestrina's models narrow-flanked, and Renoir's palette "subfusc." His most subtle ironic attack comes with his description of the erotic motive in *Pickwick Papers'* Arabella Allen:

> Strange thoughts of her surge up vaguely in me as I watch her – thoughts that I cannot express in English. . . . Elle est plus vieille que les roches entre lesquelles elle s'est assise; comme le vampire elle a été fréquemment morte, et a appris les secrets du tombeau. (184-5)

The wonderful irony here is that these words, given in French because they cannot be expressed in English, are a translation of Pater's very English words used to describe the *Mona Lisa*. This same pejorative marking of the ethos of parody can be found today in, for example, the inferred intent behind Fernando Botero's bloated figures in general but, in particular, in the parodies of Rubens's portraits of his second wife. Similarly, David's famous and polished painting of Napoleon in his study is mocked by the incompleteness of Larry Rivers's painting, ironically entitled *The Greatest Homosexual*. There is even a parody of David's compositional elements: the painter's flourish of signing his name on a scroll is altered to an unromantic and unindividualizing stencil stamp.

In the light of parodies like these, it is tempting to concur with the traditional pejorative marking of the parodic ethos. But we have learned from other modern art forms that the critical distancing between the parody itself and its backgrounded text does not always lead to irony at the expense of the parodied work. Like Pope's mock epics (Paulson 1967, 6), many parodies today do not ridicule the backgrounded texts but use them as standards by which to place the contemporary under scrutiny. The modernist verse of Eliot and Pound is probably the most obvious example of this kind of attitude, one that suggests almost a respectful or deferential ethos. But, even in the nineteenth century, when the ridiculing definition of parody was most current, we have seen that this kind of reverence was often perceived as underlying the intention of parody. Hamilton's volumes of parody collections (1884-9) reveal that works are parodied in proportion to their popularity. In Isaac D'Israeli's words, "parodists do not waste their talent on obscure productions" when they offer their "playful honours" (1886, 1). From those collections, we can see that Tennyson, Browning, and Gray (for the "Elegy") are closely followed by the most revered of their predecessors: Milton and Shakespeare.

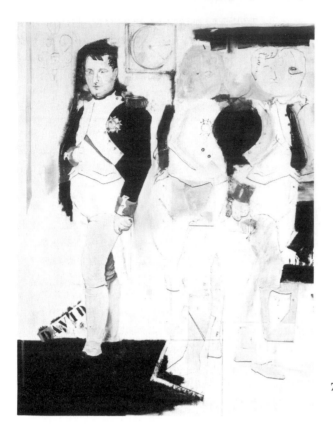

7 Larry Rivers,
*The Greatest
Homosexual*, 1964

What also becomes clear from these parodies is the reason for the retention of a rigid, negatively marked ethos for parody, despite proof to the
contrary: these respectful parodies were used to satiric ends. Once again,
the generic confusion enters. It is not Shakespeare who is being mocked
in the many topical, satiric, parodies of his best-known speeches that
appeared in *Punch* and other magazines. Satirists choose to use parodies
of the most familiar of texts as the vehicle for their satire in order to
add to the initial impact and to reinforce the ironic contrast. Jaques's
Seven Ages of Man speech from *As You Like It* (II. iii) has been used
as the form in which to launch attacks of everything from intemperance
to political ineptitude. *The Weekly Dispatch* sponsored a series of satires,
formally based on Hamlet's famous soliloquy "To be or not to be," but
aimed at the Suez Canal fiasco (5 August 1883). In none of these satires
was the parodied text ridiculed; therefore, the ethos of the parody was
not negative, even if that of the satire was.

8 Jacques-Louis David,
Napoleon in his Study

The very positive possible marking of parody's ethos is clear in the respect that many artists show in their parodic treatment of the acknowledged masterpieces of modern art. Matisse's *Goldfish*, as backgrounded by Lichtenstein's *Still Life with Gold Fish*, is not mocked, despite the alterations made: the goldfish bowl has been enlarged and centred; Matisse's own flat forms have been flattened out even more; the blank blue window in the original has been filled in with buildings taken from Matisse's earlier *Interior with Goldfish*; a detail of a Matisse-like line portrait has been added (Lipman and Marshall 1978, 87). Similarly Tom Wesselmann pays homage to Matisse in his *Great American Nude #26*. This is a parody of erotic pinups, but is also a tribute to Matisse's *Pink Nude* in its colours, pose, and rough outline. His addition of a reproduction of Matisse's *The Rumanian Blouse* allows a satiric dimension, however: the demure posture and European costume ironically comment on the seemingly shameless American nude. Similar relations of respect might be seen between Jasper Johns and Duchamp or Richard Pettibone and Stella. It is important to keep in mind, however, that this reverential variety of parody is like the more pejorative kind in one significant way: it too points to difference between texts. Although respectfully marked parody would be closer to homage than to attack, that critical distancing and marking of difference still exists.

For these reasons, the ethos postulated for parody probably should be labeled as *un*marked, with a number of possibilities for marking. In accord with the oppositional meaning of the prefix *para* (as "counter"), we can posit a challenging or contesting form of parody. This is the most common concept of the genre, the one that demands a ridiculing ethos. Examples abound in what we traditionally call parody: Offenbach's *Orpheus in the Underworld* is a parodic inversion of the serious Greek myth on the level of the libretto. On the musical level, its mocking parody of Gluck's *Orpheus and Eurydice* in the overture is underlined by the incongruous cancan melody and rhythm.

Nevertheless, we also need that other meaning of *para* as "close to" in order to account for the more respectful or deferential ethos that can be claimed, not only for much modern art, but for early liturgical parody (Freidenberg 1974, 1975) and, in some ways, even the Bakhtinian (1968) carnivalesque. The true forebear of this ethos is likely classical and Renaissance imitation. Spenser's use of Ariosto in the *Faerie Queene* is both a tribute to the master and a superseding incorporation. Because of this, his practice can be called parodic, as could, today, that of Luciano Berio in his *Sinfonia*. On the record sleeve (Columbia MS 7268), Berio explains that the third section of this work is intended as a homage to Mahler:

> It was my intention here neither to destroy Mahler (who is indestructible) nor to play out a private complex about "post-Romantic music" (I have none) nor yet to spin some enormous musical anecdote (familiar among young pianists). Quotations and references were chosen not only for their real but also for their potential relation to Mahler.

The third movement of Mahler's Second Symphony is used as a "container" for the parodic "trans-contextualization" of dozens of quotations of other composers. Berio's work is less composed than assembled in such a way as to allow for the listener's perception of difference through the mutual transformation of all the component parts.

Besides this reverential ethos of parody, there is at least one other possible marking: a more neutral or playful one, close to a zero degree of aggressivity toward either backgrounded or foregrounded text. Here the lightest of mockeries of which irony is capable is involved in the parodic signal of difference. Lichtenstein's triptych after three of Monet's views of Rouen Cathedral is perhaps an example of this marking. Lichtenstein enlarges and separates Monet's dots, thereby reversing the *pointilliste* and *tachiste* technique which lets the eye fuse bits of paint. In this ironic inversion, he mocks optical theories of painting, especially the cliché that you cannot understand a painting of this kind until you physically distance yourself from it. Another example of this playful debunking ethos would be Robert Rauschenberg's "sculpture" *Odalisk*. Its title places it in a parodic relationship to the *Odalisques* of Ingres and Matisse. The language change, as we shall soon see, is itself a signal. The work consists of a box on a post, resembling a torso and a leg, I suppose. That post is firmly anchored in or on a pillow, the traditional symbol of luxury in the earlier paintings. The sides of the box are decorated with both reproductions of classical nudes and modern pinups, and the entire box is wrapped in a harem-like veil. The final playful touch is perhaps the stuffed chicken standing on top of the box. Given the language change in the title, this is probably meant as a visualization of, or literalized pun on, the French expression for an expensive courtesan – the *poule de luxe*. What is important to keep in mind here, however, is that parody – no matter what its marking – is never a mode of parasitic symbiosis. On the formal level, it is always a paradoxical structure of contrasting synthesis, a kind of differential dependence of one text upon another.

The ethos of all three entities – parody, irony, and satire – have thus far been discussed only in some hypothetically pure state which, in fact, rarely exists in artistic practice. This is why the model is one of over-lapping and shifting circles. (Irony, as the trope used by both genres, must obviously be given the most room to move.) If, within the mocking ethos of irony, there exists a gradation – from the disdainful laugh to the knowing smile – then at the point at which irony overlaps with satire it will be that contemptuous laugh that will merge with the scornful satiric ethos (which always implies corrective intent). For example, in *Dubliners*, Joyce takes serious aim at the values and mores of a city he both loved and hated. But at no time does he ever have to articulate directly his satiric intent; he can leave it to the vehicle of his savagely evaluative irony (see Hutcheon and Butler 1981). At the other end of the ironic scale is the smirk, the knowing smile of the reader who recognizes the parodic game-playing of Stanislaw Lem, for example. Lem's *A Perfect Vacuum* (1978, 1979) contains clever Borgesian reviews of nonexistent books which parody literary conventions. Many, for instance, are gently mocking attacks on the *nouveau roman*. One, said to be the review of a novel published at the Éditions du Midi (instead of Minuit), is called *Rien du tout, ou la conséquence*. Its subject, we are informed, is the fashionable Beckettian nothingness, non-being, negation; in fact, it is about "rien du tout."

The overlapping of the ethos of the genres of parody and satire (usually involving irony as well) would result in the inference on the part of the decoder of a deflating encoded intent. With a respectfully marked parody, this might present as an acknowledgment of, or even a deference toward, the parodied text, with the deflated "target" perhaps being within the foregrounded part of the text. Chaim Soutine's homages to Rembrandt in his paintings of ox carcasses come to mind. In its contesting marking, such parodic overlapping with satire would likely lead to a cynical challenging. The formal and referential lyricism and harmony of Millet's *Angélus du soir* become ironically transformed in the modern petrified visions of Dali's illustration for *Les Chants de Maldoror* and *Archeological Reminiscences of Millet's Angelus*, and in the death mask of *L'Atavisme du crépuscule*. Of course, Dali was obsessed by this painting and even wrote a long psycho-sexual study of it (1963), because it kept appearing, intruding on his life – as a design on teacups, plates, postcards, and even cheese labels. Parody of artistic form came to be used by Dali as satire of the clichés of a consumer society. A similar overlapping of parody and satire can be seen in the work of Francis Bacon. Velázquez's stately portrait of Pope Innocent X reflects the stability, coherence, and power of a past world; Bacon's parodic versions transform the throne into a bed-like cage, making authority give way to restriction and terror.

There are two possible directions that the overlapping of parody and satire can take, since the aim of parody is intramural and that of satire is extramural – that is, social or moral. There is, on the one hand, a *type* of the *genre* parody (in Genette's (1979) terms) which is satiric, and whose target is still another form of coded discourse: Woody Allen's *Zelig* ridicules the conventions of the television and movie documentary. On the other hand, besides this satiric parody, there is parodic satire (a *type* of the *genre* satire) which aims at something outside the text, but which employs parody as a vehicle to achieve its satiric or corrective end. In a post-Nietzschean world that acknowledges the death of God, Bertolt Brecht could still parody the conveniently familiar structures of the Bible in his satiric work, *The Rise and Fall of the City of Mahagonny*. The inversion of the flight of the Israelites, of Moses as leader, and of Christ as savior is parody used with satiric intent, although (some have felt) with not a little of an implied Eliotian feeling of evoking a lost world of human dignity. The Christian context appears to be rejected, yet longed for (Speirs 1972, 162-9), in Brecht's attack on the "paradise city" of materialism. The commandments become parodic prescriptive signs in a world that normally offers "quiet, concord, whisky, women" (Brecht 1979, 2, iii, 23). Brecht may spurn the Christian model of providential transcendence, but it is the similarities between Christ and the unwitting and unwilling redeemer, Jimmy, that become more evident as the work proceeds: the impoverished Jimmy's trial has its Barabas (Toby Higgins) and, before his death, Jimmy asks for water and, after it, vinegar is brought. In addition to Brecht's structural use of parody on the level of plot, Kurt Weill's music is also parodic in its respectful but contextually ironic reworking of, appropriately, Handel's *Messiah*. The combination of the two modes of parody with the scorning ethos of satire makes this one of the clearest and most complex examples of parodic satire. Brecht himself claimed that *Mahagonny* paid "conscious tribute to the irrationality of the operatic form" with its realism undermined by music (1979, 2, iii, 87), but that his real aim was always to "change society" (90).

Is there, however, a moment at which all three of the circles of our original diagram overlap totally, eclipsing nothing? If there is, it would involve both genres, with both utilizing the ironic trope to its fullest capacity. This would be the moment of potentially maximal subversion – in both aesthetic and social terms. And it would also be the moment of supreme pragmatic overdetermination. Few works come to mind, but Swift's *A Modest Proposal* certainly does. If such a complex interaction of ethos is possible, our original simple diagram must needs be transformed, as in Figure 2.

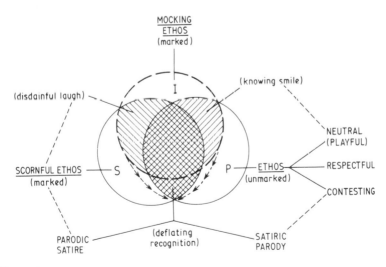

Figure 2

On the pragmatic level, we can now see more clearly that other reason for the confusion of the genres of parody and satire, the one that lies in their common use of irony. In Chapter 2, as here, the close formal and hermeneutic relationship between parody and irony was suggested. Both set up what Michael Riffaterre calls a "dialectique mémorielle" (1979b, 128) in the mind of the decoder. This is a result of their common dual superimposing structure, which nevertheless paradoxically signals difference – in semantic or textual terms. This differential dependence, or mixture of doubling and differentiation, means that parody functions intertextually as irony does intratextually: both echo in order to mark difference rather than similarity. It is this paradoxical ambivalence of irony that allows Thomas Mann to use parody to express both his respect for and his doubts about literary tradition (Heller 1958b; Honsa 1974). Yet, the interplay between *Doctor Faustus* and Goethe's *Faust* is as essentially one of difference as is the more traditionally ridiculing parody of Goethe's text found in Robert Nye's *Faust*.

A range of pragmatic ethos is often implied in those distinctions between kinds of parody: negative versus curative (Highet 1962); critical versus amusing (Lehmann 1963); affirmative versus subversive (Dane 1980). I prefer to retain the idea of a range of intended ethos, rather than that of formal opposing types of parody, because of the structural similarity underpinning all these types (repetition with critical difference). The pragmatic dimension is where the difference among types of parody lies, and concentrating on that fact might also allow for distinction rather than confusion between parody and satire: curative parody sounds perilously close to satire.

One of the clearest manifestations of the possible range of parodic ethos can be seen in the exhibition held at the Pompidou Center in Paris in the summer of 1983 that was set up in counterpointed response to the major Manet exhibition showing at the Grand-Palais at the same time. "Bonjour Monsieur Manet" did not really mock either Manet or the other show; if anything it acted as a further tribute to an artist who himself was considered a great borrower of other painters' forms. In fact, in an age of documentary naturalistic ideology, Manet was considered a pasticheur, taking the overall plan of his *Déjeuner sur l'herbe* from Raphael, and the theme itself from Titian (Clay 1983, 6). How fitting, therefore, to mount a counter-exhibition that showed how others had borrowed from and thereby come to terms with Manet himself. Often the method of supersession was parody, and the entire range of its ethos could be seen. Even more complex than the more or less respectful relationship of Matisse to Manet (Fourcade 1983) is that of Picasso (Bernadac

1983). One of Picasso's early paintings is called *Parody of Manet's Olympia*. Using the same model, but going further than Cézanne did in his *Modern Olympia* (though not as far as Robert Morris did in his "minimal performance" work, *Site*), Picasso inscribed himself in the new work and inverted the conventions of the original (themselves borrowed from Titian's *Venus of Urbino*): Olympia is black, the maid is replaced by a male friend, fruit is substituted for the flowers. In other words, the implied voyeurism of the original is ironically reworked to suggest a brothel scene. But Manet's *L'Exécution de Maximilien* (which itself echoes Goya's *Tres de Mayo*) is used somewhat differently as the backgrounded parodic structure for Picasso's *Massacres en Corée*. Here the purpose seems to be to increase the horror and the drama through ironic contrast of plural nameless massacres with individual romantic execution. Unlike the earlier, more gently mocking parody or his multiple reworkings of Velázquez's *Las Meninas*, this parodic satire has a more strongly marked negative ethos.

None of these works is really ridiculing, yet I want to call them parodies, just as their creators often did. Rosamund Tuve (1970) found herself in a similar position when trying to figure out why Herbert had called one of his poems "A Parodie." The poem made sacred a secular love poem, "Soules joy, now I am gone." In order to account for both the un-innocent title and the non-ridiculing nature of this kind of parody, Tuve turned to musical parody, both because Herbert was a musician and may have intended the poem to be put to music, and because the concept of musical parody is a much broader one. In one form, the contrafactum, it is really just a deliberate form of imitation (Verweyen 1973, 8-9). Herbert's practice is very close to what we have seen in modern parody: he remodeled familiar forms in order to say something serious with greater impact (Freeman 1963, 307).

The musical analogy to which Tuve resorted in order to account for Herbert's kind of parody is suggestive. In music, parody has two distinct meanings that recall the range of parodic ethos we have been examining. Its first meaning is closer to the respectful ethos of parody or even to the Renaissance practice of imitation. As a genre, musical parody is an acknowledged reworking of pre-existent material, but with no ridiculing intent. The *New Grove Dictionary of Music and Musicians* defines parody in this sense as a genuinely re-creative exercise in free variation. We have seen that parody has once again become important in modern music, but one element must be stressed, one that would reinforce the definition of parody as repetition, but repetition with difference: in musical parody like Stravinsky's *Pulcinella*, there is a distance between the model and

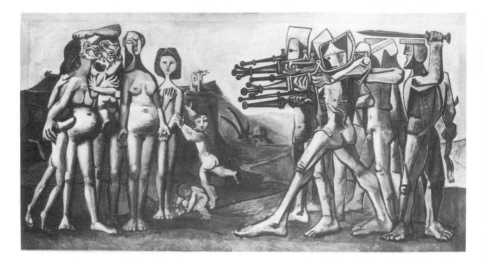

9 Pablo Picasso, *Massacres en Corée*, 1950

10 Édouard Manet, *L'Exécution de Maximilien*, 1867

the parody that is created by a stylistic dichotomy. This is even true of the reverential ethos of parody in music: Prokofiev paid tribute to the wit and urbanity of Haydn and others in his "Classical" Symphony, but there is still a sense of difference.

This is more evident in the second, non-generic meaning of musical parody – the more traditional notion of a composition with humorous intent. Frequently this type of parody in music, as in the other arts, is a limited phenomenon, usually restricting itself to quoting isolated themes, rhythms, chords, and so on, instead of the more global reworking to fuse old and new elements that characterizes both sixteenth-century and modern musical parody. In this more traditional kind of parody, recognizable noble turns of phrase will often be applied to inappropriate subjects, as when Debussy recalls *Tristan und Isolde* in his *Golliwog's Cake Walk*. As in literature or painting, this kind of parody is frequently conservative in impulse, exaggerating stylistic idiosyncrasies. The range of parodic ethos allows for everything from playful amusement (Dudley Moore's variations on the "Colonel Bogey" march in *Beyond the Fringe*) to love and respect (Victor Borge's famous Gala Concerts), even within this second meaning of musical parody.

The first, however, is potentially the more fruitful here: parody as the transmuting and remodeling of existing musical forms (Finscher and Dadelsen 1962, 815) without any specifying of ridiculing intent. This does not mean that ridicule is not possible. On the contrary, it is one of a range of possible ethos or intended responses. That other artists besides Herbert may have had a musical notion of parody is suggested by the parodist John Barth's remark, recalling his early training in music at the Juilliard:

> At heart I'm an arranger still, whose chiefest literary pleasure is to take a received melody – an old narrative poem, a classical myth, a shopworn literary convention, a shard of my experience, a New York Times Book Review series – and, improvising like a jazzman within its constraints, reorchestrate it to present purpose. (1982, 30)

Part of that present purpose is to show difference, ironic difference, as much as similarity.

Irony can be both including and excluding; it suggests both complicity and distance. In this it resembles the functioning of laughter, both socially (Dupréel 1928, 228-31) and psychologically (Levine 1969, 168). But to say this is not to equate it with laughter or ridicule. Irony, in demanding shared codes for comprehension, can be as exclusive a strategy as ridicule. It is as potentially conservative a force as corrective, deriding laughter. Parody, which deploys irony in order to establish the critical distance necessary to its formal definition, also betrays a tendency toward conservatism, despite the fact that it has been hailed as the paradigm of aesthetic revolution and historical change. It is to this paradox of parody that we now turn.

4

THE PARADOX OF PARODY

---

a vile art *Matthew Arnold*

a noble art *Sir Owen Seaman*

Overtly imitating art more than life, parody self-consciously and self-critically points us to its own nature. But, while it is true that parody invites a more literal and literary reading of a text, it is by no means unrelated to what Edward Said (1983) calls the "world," because the entire act of the *énonciation* is involved in the activation of parody. The ideological status of parody is a subtle one: the textual and pragmatic natures of parody imply, at one and the same time, authority and transgression, and both now must be taken into account. To use the categories of philosophical logic, the language of parodic texts subverts the traditional mention/usage distinction: that is, it refers both to itself and to that which it designates or parodies. Because parody is so overtly interdiscursive and "two-voiced," it is not surprising that we have been witnessing lately a revalorizing of the work of Mikhail Bakhtin, the formulator of literary polyphony and of dialogism, for whom parody is "an intentional dialogized hybrid. Within it, languages and styles actively and mutually illuminate one another" (1981, 76). For Bakhtin, parody is a relativizing, depriviling mode. We have seen that, according to Todorov's (1981, 110) systematization of Bakhtin's unsystematic terminology, parody is a divergent, passive, diphonic form of represented discourse.

Given that Bakhtin privileged the novel genre, this chapter will for the most part retain that generic focus. There is another reason for this limitation, however, and that is my conviction that many of the fictional narrative forms of today are, in fact, a very extreme and self-conscious version of the novel as defined by Bakhtin himself: as a parodic self-reflexive, non-monologic form. Yet modern parody in general and most modern fiction fell under Bakhtin's severest strictures. The question is: why? There is no doubt that some theories of the novel could be said to be self-restricting in the sense that they must logically terminate in the valorizing of one particular form. Auerbach, for instance, wrote *Mimesis* (1957) from the implied stance that nineteenth-century French realism is the only true realism, and therefore that all attempts before Stendhal are but imperfect steps *en route,* and that any after are signs of its decline. Brecht (1974) accused Lukács of making a fetish of one historically relative literary form – the same nineteenth-century realist fiction – and then dogmatically demanding that all other art conform to this model. And Ian Watt (1966) so narrows his normative definition of the novel genre that he ends up leaving room only for one real novelist – Samuel Richardson. Only one modern novelist escaped Bakhtin's disapproval of post-Renaissance literature: Dostoevsky. Yet, unlike the other critics mentioned, Bakhtin presents us with a paradox: his various "theories," if we can call such deliberate unsystematizing by such a name, are potentially much more plural and open. It is his own statements of application that threaten to place limits upon the concepts' viability. To *adopt* slavishly Bakhtin's specific statements about parody (that is, to imitate his practice) is to fall victim to the arbitrary and monolithic, not to say monologic, in those statements; to *adapt,* on the other hand, is to open up one of the most suggestive Pandora's boxes this century has produced.

From Bakhtin's box could emerge a plethora of refreshing approaches to a new corpus, especially modernist and postmodernist literature, since both are frequently parodic in form and intent. Yet Bakhtin himself had few good words for modern parody:

> in modern times the functions of parody are narrow and unproductive. Parody has grown sickly, its place in modern literature is insignificant. We live, write and speak today in a world of free and democratized language; the complex and multi-leveled hierarchy of discourses, forms, images, styles that used to permeate the entire system of official language and linguistic consciousness was swept away by the linguistic revolution of the Renaissance.
> (1981, 71)

But we have been noticing that today our cultural forms are more rather than less self-reflecting and parodic than ever. Perhaps, then, we do not, *pace* the utopian Bakhtin, live or write today in a linguistic context that is free and democratic. Certainly the radical Italian poets and novelists of the early sixties, whose rallying cry was *asemanticità*, led the attack against what they saw as the linguistic reification caused by bourgeois neocapitalism (Manganelli 1967). Perhaps our language is democratized today only in the sense that it has been totally bureaucratized. But then the battle would still be against an official language – a battle, that is, against uniform meaningless babble (an inverted Babel). Perhaps, then, we are witnessing today, in the revival of parodic forms, the preparation of a new linguistic and literary consciousness comparable to the role parody played, according to Bakhtin, in medieval and Renaissance society.

In fact, one could argue that the interest in Bakhtin today does not stem originally from any mechanical application of his theories, but rather from the relevance to the contemporary in his remarks on medieval and Renaissance literature and society. It is important, however, to recognize the implications of Bakhtin's historical and local context in order to understand his rejection of the contemporary. In other words, we must not forget that it was contemporary literature that his formalist and Marxist coevals were promoting. While this is a natural self-distinguishing reaction on Bakhtin's part, we should not today accept those strictures as law, for that would be to ignore Bakhtin's own lesson of the singular historicity of every utterance. We should look to what the theories suggest, rather than what the practice denies, for within the very unsystematic and often vague nature of those theories lies their power of suggestion and provocation.

(A brief example will illustrate this tension in Bakhtin between theory and practice, between suggestiveness and restriction. In *The Political Unconscious* (1981), Fredric Jameson seems to feel that Bakhtin works in a specialized context only (specific moments of carnival). Therefore Jameson seeks to expand dialogism into the structure of class discourse by adding the qualification that "the normal form of the dialogic is essentially an *antagonistic* one" (84). But, in the theoretical discussion in his work on Dostoevsky, Bakhtin makes clear that disputation is by definition part of the dialogic relationship (1973, 152). Nevertheless, when he does look at a specific situation (Renaissance or medieval carnival), in practice, the negative pole of dialogic "ambivalence" falls away. Bakhtin's utopian tendency is always to collapse the negative into the positive: death gives way to rebirth; scatology and obscenity reaffirm the vital body. Jameson is attracted to just this utopian impulse in Bakhtin, but – reacting to the overwhelmingly positive tone of his practice – feels the need to add a negative pole to create a true antagonistic relationship. Yet Bakhtin's theory already includes this structure.)

It is his theory, then, that would allow for a fruitful approach (both formal and ideological) to that modern corpus which his practice would have rejected. Contemporary metafiction is decidedly characterized by a very Bakhtinian, ironic use of parodic forms: we at once think of the works of John Fowles or John Barth and their overt historical development from prior literary forms. Bakhtin argued that the European prose novel was born and developed through a process of free and transforming translation of the works of others (Bakhtin 1978, 193). He also felt that the novel was unique as a genre in its ability to internalize or constitute a self-criticism of its own form (444). The novel that he prized so much for this autocritical faculty, *Don Quijote*, could easily be seen as the direct forebear of the contemporary metafictional investigations into the relation of discourse to reality. Furthermore, today's auto-representational novels, because of their use of parody, are even more overtly and functionally polyphonic in structure and style than Dostoevsky's work ever was.

It is Bakhtin's theory, if not always his practice, that allows for looking at parody as a form of "double-directed" discourse (1973, 153). Recent theorists of intertextuality have argued that such intertextual dialogism is a constant of all avant-garde literature. According to Laurent Jenny (1976, 279), the role of self-consciously revolutionary texts is to rework those discourses whose weight has become tyrannical. This is not imitation; it is not a monologic mastery of another's discourse. It is a dialogic, parodic reappropriation of the past. Postmodernist metafiction's parody and the ironic rhetorical strategies that it deploys are perhaps the clearest modern examples of the Bakhtinian "double-voiced" word. Their dual textual and semantic orientation makes them central to Bakhtin's ([Bakhtin] Vološinov 1973, 115) concept of "reported speech" as discourse *within* and *about* discourse – not a bad definition of metafiction. The two textual voices of ironic and parodic fiction combine dialogically; they do not cancel each other out. In both Bakhtin's philosophy of alterity and his formal dialogic model, there is radical separation, despite mediation. (Perhaps in such a concept lies the possibility of a new approach to a feminist discourse of the muted and the dominant (Booth 1982; Showalter 1981).)

Like Bakhtin's Renaissance and medieval carnival (Bakhtin 1968) (and, we might add, like the 1970s performance art), modern metafiction exists on the self-conscious borderline between art and life, making little formal distinction between actor and spectator, between author and co-creating reader (Hutcheon 1980). The second, joyous, inverted world of the carnival, according to Bakhtin, existed in opposition to official, serious, ecclesiastical culture, just as metafiction today contests the novelistic illusion of realist dogma and attempts to subvert a critical authoritarian-ism (by containing within itself its own first critical commentary). The ambivalence and incompleteness of contemporary novels recall the similar qualities of the carnival and of the Romantic grotesque, as defined by Bakhtin. In a novel like Leonard Cohen's *Beautiful Losers,* the social and literary inversions are typically carnivalesque: the religion of the spirit gives way to the religion of the flesh, complete with its own saints (sexy movie stars) and sacred texts (pornography and sex manuals). The official church discourse – specifically that of prayer and of the Jesuit chronicles – is parodically inverted in form and content. There is a specific and wholesale transfer from the elevated, spiritual, ideal plane to the material and bodily reality of life.

It is in this sort of way that, despite the limitations of Bakhtin's view of modern parody, many of his theoretical observations on the early carnival are surprisingly appropriate and illuminating with regard to the contemporary aesthetic and social situation. There are, perhaps, historical reasons for this ready adaptability. Contemporary metafiction, as we have seen, exists – as does the carnival – on that boundary between literature and life, denying frames and footlights. As such, it partakes of the "new performance system" of postmodernism (Benamou 1977, 6). Both its form and content can operate to subvert formalistic, logical, authoritarian structures. The ambivalent openness of contemporary fic-tion also suggests, perhaps, that the medieval and modern worlds may not be as fundamentally different as we might like to think. The car-nivalesque inversions of norms could well share a common source with subversive metafictional challenges to novelistic conventions: feelings of insecurity in the face of both nature and the social order. Fear is the emotion that contributes most to the power and seriousness of official culture, according to Bakhtin. Today we live in fear of the consequences of what our forefathers unironically called "progress": urbanization, technology, and so on. We too have developed "popular-festive" forms in response to this. But we call our folk culture "pop" today; Andy Warhol, the Rolling Stones, or the punk phenomenon signal urban protest.

However, there is today one very significant divergence from Bakhtin's view of the medieval world: unfortunately, we have not witnessed – not yet, at least – what the Marxist utopian Bakhtin called "the victory of the people" and the rebirth of a new popular "immortality" (1968, 256). Instead, our pop culture, for all its admitted vitality, still appears to represent instead our increased alienation. Novelists and poets like Leonard Cohen deliberately become pop singers in an attempt to reach the people but, even then, ironic pessimism replaces Bakhtin's optimistic utopianism. His positive view of ambivalence and incompletion often becomes negativized today, as these change into anarchy and confusion.

This ironic reversal of Bakhtin's confident perspective should act as a warning to us in our attempts to apply Bakhtin's theories to contemporary culture. We must remind ourselves that his own concepts are always rooted in history, in the specificity of time and place. Nevertheless, in discussing the particular case of the medieval carnival, Bakhtin seems to have uncovered what I believe to be another underlying principle of all parodic discourse: the paradox of its authorized transgression of norms. Bakhtin describes the subversive carnival as actually being "consecrated by tradition," both social and ecclesiastical (1968, 5). Therefore, although this popular festival and its manifest forms exist apart from "serious official, ecclesiastical, feudal, and political cult forms and ceremonials" (5), in so being, they in fact also posit those very norms. The recognition of the inverted world still requires a knowledge of the order of the world which it inverts and, in a sense, incorporates. The motivation and the form of the carnivalesque are both derived from authority: the second life of the carnival has meaning only in relation to the official first life. However, Bakhtin writes: "While carnival lasts, there is no other life outside it" (7). True, perhaps; but that "while" is significant. The medieval church may have tolerated, legalized, perhaps even preserved or created, the carnivalesque forms, but it did so only for a permitted length of time. In Bakhtin's terms: "As opposed to the official feast, one might say that carnival celebrated temporary liberation from the prevailing truth and from the established order; it marked the suspension of all hierarchical rank, privileges, norms, and prohibitions" (10). Note that he said "temporary" "suspension" and not permanent destruction of "prevailing" norms. The social inversions (such as the crowning of fools) and the parodic literary ones were both temporary transgressions, and the laughter at their expense "was absolutely unofficial but nevertheless legalized" (89). Parodic disguise was used to hide, not destroy, the sacred Word (1978, 429): Bakhtin cites a fifteenth-century theological statement which admits that "we permit folly on certain days so that we may later return with greater zeal to the service of God" (1968, 75). Centuries later, William Hone was acquitted on blasphemy charges (against his parody of the Scriptures in a political satire) on the grounds that he had not, in fact, ridiculed the Bible at all. His transgression, in other words, was authorized in yet another sense (Priestman 1980, 20).

This paradox of legalized though unofficial subversion is characteristic of all parodic discourse insofar as parody posits, as a prerequisite to its very existence, a certain aesthetic institutionalization which entails the acknowledgement of recognizable, stable forms and conventions. These function as norms or as rules which can – and therefore, of course, shall – be broken. The parodic text is granted a special licence to transgress the limits of convention, but, as in the carnival, it can do so only temporarily and only within the controlled confines authorized by the text parodied – that is, quite simply, within the confines dictated by "recognizability." While Roland Barthes (1974, 45) argued that any textual multivalence was in effect a transgression of propriety, it was this particularly legitimized quality of parodic multivalence that caused him to denigrate parody as a "classic" discourse, his version of Kristeva's (1969) "consolidation de la loi." (In Bakhtin's name, Kristeva has sought to denigrate parody. She contrasts what she sees as Bakhtin's theory of *"transgression giving itself a law"* to parodic literature's principle of *"law anticipating its own transgression"* (Kristeva 1980a, 71). That latter phrase, however, is as descriptive of Bakhtin's work as the former.)

Parody can also be seen, however, to be a threatening, even anarchic force, one that puts into question the legitimacy of other texts. It "disrealizes and dethrones literary norms" (Shlonsky 1966, 799). On another level, appropriation (borrowing or pirating) of the property of others questions art's accepted status as individualized commodity (Buchloh 1983, 191). Nevertheless, parody's transgressions ultimately remain authorized – authorized by the very norm it seeks to subvert. Even in mocking, parody reinforces; in formal terms, it inscribes the mocked conventions onto itself, thereby guaranteeing their continued existence. It is in this sense that parody is the custodian of the artistic legacy, defining not only where art is, but where it has come from. To be a custodian, however, as Post-Modernist architecture has revealed, can be a revolutionary position; the point is that is *need* not be.

The best historical model of this paradoxical process of authorized transgression in parody might be the Greek satyr play. This was performed after a trilogy of tragedies, and essentially it reworked, in comic form, the serious material of the three plays preceding it. This satyr play was thus legitimized and made as canonical as the tragedies themselves (Bakhtin 1978, 412). Likewise, in the Christian context, the authority behind the early *parodia sacra* had a particular force, since the authority was the Word of God or of His representatives on earth. Parody is, therefore, not only repetition; its imitation always entails differentiation (Genette 1979, 84), and its legitimizing authority depends on its anteriority for its status. It is this conjunction of repetition and priority that has led to those psychoanalytic illuminations of parody and imitation

(Bloom 1973; Compagnon 1979, 395). Clearly the nature of the legitimizing authority in parody is a complicated issue.

   Sometimes the work parodied is a laughable, pretentious one that begs
deflating; but even more often it is very successful works that inspire
parodies. Often the number of parodies attests to a pervasive influence
(Josephson 1975). Fifteen different parodies of Zola's *L'Assommoir*
appeared on stage in the first eight months of 1879, including one by
Zola himself (Morgan and Pagès 1980). In the eighteenth and nineteenth
centuries, parodies of the most popular operas often appeared on stage
contemporaneously with the original. Weber's *Der Freischütz* (1821) was
parodied in 1824 by *Samiel, oder die Wunderpille.* This German parody
was translated into Danish and Swedish – an obvious sign of its popularity. In the same year, an English parody was staged at Edinburgh called
*"Der Freischütz," a new muse-sick-all and see-nick performance from
the new German uproar.* The popular operas of Wagner seemed especially
prone to parody: *Tannhäuser* (1845) was taken on by the French in the
not very subtly named *Ya-Mein-Herr, Cacophonie de l'Avenir, en 3 actes
entr'acte mêlée de chants, de harpes et de chiens savants.* His *Tristan
und Isolde* was parodied by *Tristanderl und Süssholde* before it was even
staged (Rosenthal and Warrack 1964, 301-2). To some critics, parody
makes the original lose in power, appear less commanding; to others
the parody is the superior form because it does everything the original
does – and more. There is no doubt that this latter kind of audience or
reader would revel in nineteenth-century opera or in the literature of
turn-of-century France or contemporary America, while others find all
such overcoded discourse to be a sign of decadence.

   This contradictory reaction is not, however, just a matter of personal
taste. Its roots lie in the bi-directionality of the legitimacy of parody itself.
The presupposition of both a law and its transgression bifurcates the
impulse of parody: it can be normative and conservative, or it can be
provocative and revolutionary. Its potentially conservative impulse can
be seen in both extremes of the range of ethos, reverence and mockery:
parody can suggest a "complicity with high culture. . . which is merely
a deceptively off-hand way of showing a profound respect for classical-
national values" (Barthes 1972b, 119), or it can appear as a parasitical
form, mocking novelty in the hope of precipitating its destruction (and,
by implication, its own). Yet parody can, like the carnival, also challenge
norms in order to renovate, to renew. In Bakhtin's terminology, parody
can be centripetal – that is, a homogenizing, hierarchicizing influence.
But it can also be a centrifugal, de-normatizing one. And I think it is
the paradox of its authorized transgression that is at the root of this

apparent contradiction. Parody is normative in its identification with the Other, but it is contesting in its Oedipal need to distinguish itself from the prior Other.

This ambivalence set up between conservative repetition and revolutionary difference is part of the very paradoxical essence of parody; so, it is not surprising that critics should disagree on the intent of parody. As we saw in the previous chapter, there are many possible forms of the ethos of parody: is it intended as innocently reverential? ridiculing? didactic? mnemonic? ironic? Does it accept or resist the Other? In any case, of course, the very act of parodying invests the Other with both authority and an exchange value in relation to literary norms. These norms are like social ones in the sense that they are human constructs which are authoritative only to those who have constructed or at least accepted them as *a priori*. From Chaucer to Ben Jonson, through to the nineteenth-century Smith Brothers, parodies were used in English literature as a means of control of excesses in literary fashion; the rise of avant-garde forms, in particular, gave these writers something upon which to exercise their parodic conservatism. Nineteenth-century British parody has been said to represent "the college man's wittily expressed dislike of the art that either in sentiment or technique departs too markedly from the cultured tradition of the tribe" (Kitchin 1931, 298). It is clear that literary norms depend upon some degree of social and cultural homogeneity. This is true in other senses as well. While comedy had once been accepted as an ethically responsible literary form, nineteenth-century English critics (like Matthew Arnold), who felt poetry carried an ethical message, did not take kindly to parody, for it appeared to subvert the dignity of art.

The conservative impulse of parody raises a very important general question. To what extent can we separate literary judgments from projected social or ideological ones? Northrop Frye denies the very possibility:

> Every deliberately constructed hierarchy of values in literature known to me is based on a concealed social, moral, or intellectual analogy. This applies whether the analogy is conservative and Romantic, as it is in Arnold, or radical, giving the top place to comedy, satire, and the values of prose and reason, as it is in Bernard Shaw. (1970, 23)

The fact that we have trouble separating aesthetic and ideological value judgments is reflected directly in that taxonomic confusion we have seen between literary parody and social satire, a confusion that persists in much literary criticism (see, for example, Rose 1979, 44-5). Bakhtin (1978, 414) was right to point out that Greek parody did not operate on heroes and wars, but on their literary "heroicization" (epic or tragic). In other words, the flaws, errors, and absurdities that parody often reveals in its content (or in the moral implications of its form) are satiric. If, in nineteenth-century Cambridge, parody at times resembled a gentlemanly homage, in the previous centuries it had also proved to be a potent political weapon. Satire and parody, as we have seen, have a natural affinity for each other. To use Frye's (1970, 229) wonderful terms, cranks with new ideas, or established conventions invented by dead cranks, provide particularly enticing targets for literary parody and social satire, both separately and together. As an example, we need only think of a piece of popular music like Jimi Hendrix's rock version of "The Star-Spangled Banner." In the context of the Vietnam War protest, the modulation in the song from a parodic distortion of the mutilated glory of the American national anthem to the appropriately ironic military melody of "The Last Post" was obviously satirically intended.

It is perhaps not surprising, then, that there has been a close historical connection between political censorship and the denigration of parody. Because satire often uses parodic literary forms, parody is often officially trivialized in order to muzzle its satire's subversive criticism (Rose 1979, 31-2, 169). I do not mean to suggest that parody is only literary or artistic satire: the range of tone and intent of parody, as we saw in the last chapter, is far more extensive than such a view would permit. Parody, rather, invokes a self-conscious critical distancing of the Other which *can* be used as one of the rhetorical mechanisms to signal the reader to seek immanent, if indirect, ideal standards whose deviation is to be satirically condemned in the work. In a sense Nabokov was correct in saying: "Satire is a lesson, parody is a game" (1973, 75). Satire does not authorize but ridicules the transgression of social norms, though it may parodically legitimize literary ones.

A good example might be Fielding's novel *Joseph Andrews*, which has often been called a parody of Richardson's *Pamela*. I would suggest, however, that it is in fact a satiric parody of *Pamela* and a respectful parody of *Don Quijote* (its subtitle is "written in the manner of Cervantes"). Like his other work, *Shamela*, Fielding's *Joseph Andrews* satirizes Richardson's middle-class assumptions. In tilting ever so slightly each equivocal expression or situation in *Pamela*, Fielding reveals the vulgarity of the girl he judges to be a conniving wench. It is also true, of course, that, in parodying a certain style of writing, an author like Swift can satirize the mental and literary habits implied in that manner. Chaucer's "Rime of Sir Thopas" is a parody of metrical romances, but it is also a satire of the social institution behind the chivalric system.

In Jane Austen's early work, there is a tension between her desire to exorcize the naïve clichés of sentimental "women's" fiction and her unwillingness or inability to do so. Susan Gubar has argued that the best way for Austen to indict the literary and social patriarchy was to *seem* inoffensive. For example, in *Northanger Abbey*, Austen parodies gothic conventions, while still relying on them for her novel's shape. As a result she succeeds in reinvesting the "female gothic" with authority derived from the interaction of parody and satire: the true cause of women's confinement is shown not to be walls or financial dependency but miseducation – a lesson Emily Brontë's Isabella of *Wuthering Heights* illustrates tragically (Gilbert and Gubar 1979, 123-35, 288). Satire tends to defend norms; it ridicules in order to bring deviation into line – or it used to. "Black humor," today's most common form of satire, seems to many to be a defensive humor of shock, a humor of lost norms, of disorientation, of lost confidence (Dooley 1971).

The problem here lies in the fact that, in order to question either literary or social norms, a writer has to be able to assume a certain cultural homogeneity, as we shall see in more detail in the next chapter. However, from this requirement stems the fact that some parodies and most satires can "date" more or less quickly. Both the interrelations of the two genres and their historical limitations or frames of reference will be clearer if we look at a brief example that elicits, in fact almost demands, the literary and ideological competences of a specifically British reader. Ideally, the reader of Wendy Cope's parody of Shakespeare's famous Sonnet 55 should be aware not only of contemporary English social institutions, but also of the literary fact that Shakespeare's sonnets are themselves often parodic of the Petrarchan and classical traditions. We recall Sonnet 55:

> Not marble, nor the gilded monuments
> Of princes, shall outlive this powerful rhyme;
> But you shall shine more bright in these contents
> Than unswept stone, besmeared with sluttish time.
> When wasteful war shall statues overturn,
> And broils root out the work of masonry,
> Nor Mars his sword nor war's quick fire shall burn
> The living record of your memory.
> 'Gainst death and all-oblivious enmity
> Shall you pace forth; your praise shall still find room
> Even in the eyes of all posterity
> That wear this world out to the ending doom.
> So, till the judgment that yourself arise,
> You live in this, and dwell in lovers' eyes.

Cope's parody is:

> Not only marble, but the plastic toys
> From cornflakes packets will outlive this rhyme:
> I can't immortalize you, love – our joys
> Will lie unnoticed in the vault of time.
> When Mrs Thatcher has been cast in bronze
> And her administration is a page
> In some O-level text book, when the dons
> Have analysed the story of our age,
> When travel firms sell tours of outer space
> And aeroplanes take off without a sound
> And Tulse Hill has become a trendy place
> And Upper Norwood's on the underground
> Your beauty and my name will be forgotten –
> My love is true, but all my verse is rotten.

The particular interaction of the satiric and social with the parodic and literary in this brief example is paradigmatic. Marshall McLuhan also pointed out that when "Dryden drew a parallel to the Old Testament narrative of King David and Absalom in his *Absalom and Achitophel* he was creating a parallel between the contemporary and the past which lent a great force to the political critique of the present" (McLuhan and Watson 1970, 168-9). The neoclassical mock epic in general, in fact, is just such a recasting of epic forms for satiric purposes – directed, however, not against the epic model but against contemporary customs or politics.

To move from these examples of parody's potential conservatism to the situation created by contemporary metafiction is to feel as if today we really are at what Robert Scholes (1969, 269) called "an ideological watershed," one comparable to the one at the end of Bakhtin's favorite period, the end of the Middle Ages and the start of the Renaissance. But that earlier (conservative?) confidence in human modes of knowing, understanding, controlling, and even surviving seems to be lacking today. Along with this has disappeared our ability or willingness to establish, with any sureness, hierarchies of value, either aesthetic or social. The "elitism" on both of these levels that characterized literary modernism – its respect for form and craft, and also for both reason and psychological "truth" – has been challenged by postmodernist literature. The conservative value of control has given way to what some feel to be anarchy and randomness (Hoffmann, Hornung, Kunow 1977).

Certainly one of the most manifest forms of parodic contestation of modernist "elitism" or, better, academicism has been the attempt on the part of recent fiction to destroy the Arnoldian, nineteenth-century separation between high and low culture, restoring to literature "an awareness of the sexual-, racial-, and class-content (and function) of all art" (Pütz 1973, 233). The potential social and intellectual gap between author and reader is supposed to be closed or at least lessened by a novel which overtly acknowledges that it only exists insofar as (and while) it is read, and that it must be read against a background of accessible (because textually incorporated) culture. Typical of this new kind of high/low self-reflexive fiction is the parodic work of Tom Robbins. There are two epigraphs to his *Even Cowgirls Get the Blues*, one from William Blake and one from Roy Rogers. If all the arts are part of the same culture today, it is because the popular arts have become internalized, incorporated into the serious forms, democratizing the class-inspired hierarchies of an earlier time. In this sense, then, we may indeed be witnessing a variety of (or variation on) Bakhtin's carnivalesque parodic inversion and the triumph of the people.

The novel today has been one of many art forms that has turned to popular art and culture for this democratization and potential revitalization. This is not surprising, since the novel itself was one of the first middle-class or (in eighteenth-century terms) popular forms of literature. Like Bakhtin's "popular-festive" folk forms of the Middle Ages and the Renaissance, the pop art forms used in contemporary fiction are parodically subversive of elitist, highbrow concepts of literature: we find comic books, Hollywood movies, popular songs, pornography, and so on, being used parodically in novels today. However, these transgressions of literary and social norms, for all their revolutionary suggestion, could be said to remain legalized by authority, just as pop music is made popular not by the youths who buy it as much as by the authorities that manipulate their consumption – New York publishers and marketing experts (who both pre-censor and peddle), multinational record companies, and even commercial radio stations.

The contemporary novel that parodically incorporates high and low art forms is another variant of what Bakhtin valued in fiction, the dialogic or polyphonic. Tom Robbins inverts the literary and social conventions of the popular western genre to give us the Rubber Rose Ranch ("the largest all-girl ranch in the West"), a citified New York Indian, and a very un-chaste and un-manly concept of (cowgirl) love as lesbian sexual play. Similarly the (celibate) relationship between the cowboy and his horse that is at the core of the heroic western is subverted in Robert Kroetsch's parody, in *The Studhorse Man*, by Hazard Lepage's obsession with equine fertility. Margaret Atwood's incorporation, in *Lady Oracle*, of the structures and conventions of both the "costume gothic" or popular romance, and modern, hermetic, serious verse, works in much the same way as does Bakhtinian parody in its motivation and form, in its authorized subversion of social and literary norms. The same is true of Hubert Aquin's use of the structure of the popular spy thriller in *Prochain Episode*. Borges, Robbe-Grillet, and Nabokov are only a few of those who use parodic versions of detective-story structures; Calvino, Carpentier, and others use fantasy and science-fiction modes. Another form that acts as a frequent parodic model is that of pornography, a popular art (of sorts) that makes critics even more uneasy than ever, although it is precisely this erotic form that Bakhtin's insights on the carnival's valorization of the "material bodily lower stratum" illuminate best (Hutcheon 1983, 88-92).

These are all highly conventionalized forms which become either overt or covert models within metafictional works, models that act as narrative clichés which signal to the reader the presence of textual auto-representation. While parody clearly asserts this kind of aesthetic self-reflexivity, it is not the only mechanism of auto-referentiality today. There is a danger of using parody as the paradigm of self-reflexiveness, as we saw in Chapter 1 with Margaret Rose's *Parody//Metafiction* (1979). She has obviously been influenced by Bakhtin, who saw the novel's polyphonic form as differing from the monologic epic in its overt rejection of any claim to authority or absoluteness of meaning or language. It is true that the self-conscious novel today does what parody has always had the potential to do: that is, in one novelist's words, "to displace, energize, and re-embody its criticism – to literally reunite it with our experience of the text" (Sukenick 1975, 430). Modern metafiction is both dialogic and truly parodic to a greater and more explicit degree than Bakhtin could have recognized. As with his prized *Don Quijote*, today's self-referential fiction has the potential to be an "auto-critique" of discourse in its relation to reality. In saying this, we must remind ourselves once again, however, that there is no necessary correlation between self-criticism and radical ideological change.

However, like the sixteenth century, the postmodern period has witnessed a proliferation of parody as one of the modes of positive aesthetic self-reference as well as conservative mockery. Perhaps parody can flourish today because we live in a technological world in which culture has replaced nature as the subject of art (Hughes 1980, 324). One of the things that these two widely separated periods have in common, I suggested earlier, is the sense of ideological instability, of a challenging of norms. But parody today can be both progressive and regressive (Shlonsky 1966, 801). Bakhtin felt that early parody prepared the way for the novel by distancing language from reality, by making overt the artifice that in fact defines all art. What we are reading today in the works of those obsessively parodic and encyclopedic metafictionists – from Jorge Luis Borges to Italo Calvino, from John Fowles to Umberto Eco – is the logical result of this view of the novel's engendering. But all of their parodic transgressions remain legitimized, authorized by their very act of inscribing the backgrounded parodied text, albeit with critical distancing of various degrees.

What happens when an *un*authorized transgression occurs? I suspect it would have to go beyond even the interlingual and intertextual play of Nabokov's *Ada*. Perhaps it would begin something like this: "river-run, past Eve and Adam's, from swerve to shore to bend of bay, brings us by a commodius vicus of recirculation back to Howth Castle and Environs" (Joyce 1959, 3). Joyce's *Finnegans Wake* is more than just an extreme of parody or self-reflexivity. It is not just a distortion. Here, I think, we come the closest to total subversion that is possible within the elastic confines of comprehension. This is not temporary legitimate *inversion*; it is closer to permanent *perversion* – which aims at *conversion*. Joyce's "last word in stolen telling," then, might sound like this: "A way a lone a last a loved a long the" . . ."riverrun past Eve and Adam's. . ."

5

ENCODING AND DECODING:
THE SHARED CODES OF PARODY

> every writer *creates* his own precursors. His work modifies our
> conception of the past, as it will modify the future.
> *Jorge Luis Borges*

Is parody in the eye of the beholder? The stress on the pragmatics of
parody as well as on its formal properties has perhaps suggested that
this is the case. The recognition and interpretation of parody are obviously
central to any description of its functions. They are not, however, the
whole story. In the last chapter, the issue of *encoded intent* was indirectly
introduced through the concept of transgression of norms. One could
argue that, if there has been no satisfying theory of parody developed
up to this point, it has been because of the lack today of an adequate
theoretical framework in which to deal with that process of textual
production or encoding of parody. Perhaps the time has come to rethink
our modernist anti-Romanticism.

Despite the fact that most of our schematic models for communication
– from Jakobson (1960) to Chatman (1979) to Eco (1979) – give the initial
position of priority on the left of the diagram to the sender or encoder,
and then proceed through the text to the receiver on the right, we seem
to have considerable difficulty today, in the wake of structuralism and
post-structuralism, in discussing the producers of texts. Yet, when we
call something a parody, we posit some encoding intent to cast a critical
and differentiating eye on the artistic past, an intent that we, as readers,
then *infer* from the text's (covert or overt) inscription of it. In reaction
against a Romantic emphasis on the originating (real) creator, critical
formalism in literature has come to speak only of *implied* authors, those
implied by the text. Yet the text may imply all it likes, and the reader

still might not "get" the implication. For this reason, it is perhaps truer to our experience of reading parody to talk of the *inferred* encoder and encoding process. But this shift still does not exempt us from having to deal with the textual producer of parody, even as inferred by us as readers.

The question to be considered before we can do this, however, is the larger one of *why* we choose not to discuss the act of production in criticism today, why we consider it "old-fashioned" as a critical concept within our present "discursive model." This last term is a revision of a Foucaldian notion, put forward by Timothy Reiss in his book, *The Discourse of Modernism* (1982): at any given time or place one discursive theory is dominant and so "provides the conceptual tools that make the majority of human practices meaningful" (11). However, this prevailing theoretical model is also accompanied by a strong but occulted practice, a practice which gradually subverts the model by revealing in the theory such conflicting internal contradictions that certain forms of the practice itself begin to become tools of analysis. The dominant theory since the seventeenth century, Reiss argues, has been variously labeled as positivist, capitalist, experimentalist, historicist, or modern; Reiss calls it analytico-referential. Its suppressed practice is that of "the enunciating subject *as discursive activity*" (42). This is the broader context that is in a position to offer an explanation of why theories of parody have been hindered by the lack of a theory of production. According to Reiss, science, philosophy, and art have all worked toward the occultation of the act and responsibility of enunciation (*énonciation*); however, all three are now also becoming the site of the surfacing of that same practice and its recent subverting of notions of objectivity, of linguistic transparency, and indeed of the concept of the subject. Today's parodic art forms are one such locus of subversion.

Parody is one of the techniques of self-referentiality by which art reveals its awareness of the context-dependent nature of meaning, of the importance to signification of the circumstances surrounding any utterance. But any discursive situation, not just a parodic one, includes an enunciating addresser and encoder as well as a receiver of the text. However, in the collective name of scientific universality and objectivity, of novelistic realism, and of critical anti-Romanticism, that enunciating entity is what Reiss sees as having been suppressed – both as an individual subject and as even the inferred producer of the text. The Romantic creator, as originating and original source of meaning, may well be dead, as Barthes argued years ago (1972a, 7-8), but the creator's *position* – a position of discursive authority – remains, and increasingly is the self-conscious focus of much contemporary art. In the midst of a general dethroning of authority by the decentering of everything from the transcendental *cogito* to the economy and the instincts, parody is showing us that there is a need to look again at the interactive powers involved in the production and reception of texts. The position of authority remains, as we saw in the last chapter, and it remains to subvert the notions of objectivity and naturalness in art, as it does in "postmodern" science today (Toulmin 1982).

Once again, it is contemporary metafiction that will provide us with the clearest examples of the present investigations into these interactive powers. Here parody is frequently joined to manipulative narrative voices, overtly addressing an inscribed receiver, or covertly maneuvering the reader into a desired position from which intended meaning (recognition and then interpretation of parody, for example) can be allowed to appear, as if in anamorphic form. What is interesting is that this almost didactic self-consciousness about the *entire act* of enunciation (the production and reception of a text) has only led in much current criticism to the valorizing of the *reader*. It is true that this marks a predictable reaction against both Romantic intentionalism (author-centered) and modernist formalism (text-centered). But the ubiquitous parodic forms of today's metafiction demand a broader enunciative context.

In discussing freedom and constraint in the reading process, Jonathan Culler asserts that there "must always be dualisms: an interpreter and something to interpret" (1982, 75). But parody teaches that dualisms are not enough. This does not mean that we have to return to a Romantic interest in the extratextual intention of the god-like creator; it is more a matter of inferring the activities of an encoding agent. No longer to believe in the textual producer as a person is the first step to restoring the wholeness of the act of enunciation: we would then know an author only as a position to be filled within the text, as inferred, in other words, by us as readers. To use the terms "producer" and "receiver" of a text, then, is to speak not of individual subjects but of what could be called "subject positions" (Eagleton 1983, 119), which are not extratextual but rather are essential constitutive factors of the text, and of the parodic text in particular (see Eco 1979, 10-11). The Romantic myth is put to rest; the "writer thinks less of writing originally, and more of rewriting. The image for writing changes from original *inscription* to parallel script" (Said 1983, 135) – a change attested to by metafiction's parodic structures today. In other words, the position of the textual producer, banished by the anti-Romanticism of modernism, has been reinstated, and I would argue that the omnipresence of parodic forms in art today has played its role in this reinstatement, as has the new stress on performance, whereby "signs of the artist's. . .presence are demanded in the published work" (Rothenberg 1977, 14).

Theorists like Reiss and Foucault have finally started focusing our attention on the enunciation, in all its complexity: for them it is an act conditioned by the operation of certain modalities or laws, including the status and position of the enunciator, "a particular, vacant space that may in fact be filled by different individuals" (Foucault 1972, 96). Yet most of the theory and criticism today that deals with parody chooses to continue to ignore this position, and it usually does so in the name of intertextuality. When Julia Kristeva (1969) coined the term, she noted that there were three elements involved besides the text under consideration: the author, the reader, and the other exterior texts. These elements were arranged along two axes: a horizontal one of the dialogue of the author with his or her potential reader, and a vertical one between the text itself and the other texts. This set-up is very neat; it is possibly too neat, however, too schematic to be true to the actual experience of reading. Is the intertextual dialogue not rather one between the reader and his or her memory of other texts, as provoked by the text in question? Certainly the role of the author in any subsequent discussions of intertextuality has been suppressed, even in the work done on parody. As the work of Michael Riffaterre has made clear, from the perspective of any theory of intertextuality, the experience of literature consists only of a text, a reader, and his or her reactions, which take the form of systems of words, grouped associatively in the reader's mind. Two texts, then, could share these systems without being parodically encoded; the locus of textual appropriation here is in the reader, not the author, real or inferred. An intertext, then, would not necessarily be the same as a parodied text; it is "the corpus of texts the reader may legitimately connect with the one before his eyes, that is, the texts brought to mind by what he is reading" (Riffaterre 1980a, 626).

Most reader-oriented theories are dual-focused (reader/text) in this way, even those that deal with interpretive authority (Fish 1980). Intentions become "forms of conventional behavior that are to be conventionally 'read' " (Fish 1982, 213). But even Stanley Fish agrees that we cannot understand a text independently of intention, that is, of the "assumption that one is dealing with marks or sounds produced by an intentional being, a being situated in some enterprise in relation to which he has a purpose or a point of view" (213). As we saw in earlier chapters, the parodic text that formally incorporates its parodied material and whose pragmatic ethos is signaled by its rhetorical strategies demands that any theory pretending to account for its complexity should also deal with the *position* and *power* of the enunciating agent, the producer of the parody. We need not resort to a Hirschian view of the real author's meaning (Hirsch 1967), the view attacked in an earlier incarnation as the "intentional fallacy" by Wimsatt and Beardsley (Wimsatt 1967); it would suffice to situate the intentional acts inscribed in the text. Parody, in general, functions as do the index and commentary of Nabokov's *Pale Fire*, the list of plagiarisms in Alasdair Gray's *Lanark*, or the parodic footnotes in *Tom Jones, Tristram Shandy*, or the tenth section of Joyce's *Finnegans Wake* (Benstock 1983; Kenner 1964, 39-40): the counterpointed double-voicing calls attention to the presence of both author and reader positions within the text and to the manipulating power of some kind of "authority." The subject position of the producer of parody is that of a controlling agent whose actions account for the textual evidence: in a sense, it is a hypothetical hermeneutical construct, inferred or "postulated" (Nehemas 1981) by the reader from the text's inscription. But what if the reader "misreads" the intention? What if he or she misses the parody or substitutes for it an intertextual chain of echoes derived from his or her own reading? Can the producer of parody today assume enough of a cultural background on the part of the audience to make parody anything but a limited or, as some would say, elitist literary genre today?

Literary writers have always turned to the texts of the past, but they have not always had to be as didactic and overt as, say, John Fowles in *The French Lieutenant's Woman*. The classical practice of citing from the great works of the past was aimed at borrowing some of their prestige and authority, but, in order for that to come about, it also assumed the reader would recognize the internalized literary models and collaborate in the completing of the communication circuit – from one "learnèd memory" ("memoria dotta") to another (Conte 1974, 10). The same was probably true of the Renaissance revivals of this practice or of Dante's use of Virgil, for instance. This was intended to show the poet's respect for, and knowledge of, the tradition in which he operated, but it also depended on the competence of the reader to recognize the new possibilities Dante had added in his particular redistribution of those traditional formal elements (Contini 1970, 372-90). For both authors and readers, the past represented what Paul Zumthor has called a "continuum mémoriel," an implicit and common knowledge external to any artist's individual discourse (1976, 320). To judge from the overtness of many of our contemporary art forms, such a continuum can perhaps no longer be assumed in these days of democratized (but perhaps necessarily less particularized and uniform) education.

With any change in the audience of art, then, we are likely to be able to posit a parallel change in the expectations of those who produce parody. Where, however, does the balance of power lie today? Who is in control of whom? Is the author an elitist figure demanding a sophisticated reader? Or is the inferring reader ultimately the one with the power, the power to ignore or misread the intentions of the parodist? As Wolfgang Iser has pointed out, as soon as we are concerned with the effects of a text (the effects of ironic, evaluative mockery, reverence, and so on) as well as its meaning, we are dealing with a pragmatic use of signs that "always involves some kind of manipulation, as a response is to be elicited from the recipient of the signs" (1978, 54). If the desired response is a reaction to the recognition and interpretation of parody, then the producer of the text must guide and control the understanding of the reader. To do so as overtly as does much contemporary self-reflexive fiction is not necessarily to constrain the reader any more than more covert tactics would. As Wayne Booth (1961) taught us years ago, all writers have a rhetoric; their only choice lies in which one they use. In fact, as we shall now see, one could argue that the best way to demystify power is to reveal it in all its arbitrariness.

Take, for instance, the opening of a recent novel:

> You are about to begin reading Italo Calvino's new novel, *If on a winter's night a traveler*. Relax. Concentrate. Dispel every other thought. Let the world around you fade. Best to close the door; the TV is always on in the next room. (1981, 3)

We are ordered to sit comfortably and prepare ourselves for reading. The "you" addressed by the narrator, we assume, is us. Of course, this assumption, like many others, will prove false or, rather, false to some extent, for "you" also becomes a character (a male Reader) in this amusing parody of the standard love story. Calvino's overt manipulation of the readers (us and him) allegorically demonstrates the presence and power of the authorial *position*, though its very obviousness and our realization of the different readers involved work to undercut that power and call it into question. The narrator's directive remarks are balanced by the realization in chapter 8 by the novelist character, Silas Flannery, of the tyranny of both reader expectation and reader control: like us, she (in this case, definitely thematized as a female Other Reader) can choose not to read, to stop reading, to buy another book, and so on.

Yet what kind of reader is required by the whole of this complex parodic text that Calvino has produced? Not only does he write stylistic parodies (not imitations, for ironic, critical distance is evident) of many types of narratives, from Japanese erotica to Pasternak, but he also parodies other coded systems (from the Derridian theory of the trace and erasure to the Barthesian concern with the pleasure or *jouissance* of the text). The entire novel is structured parodically on the genres of the detective story and thriller. Its title ironically recalls that other book that provides many beginnings of tales: the *Thousand and One Nights*. The irony lies in that the earlier text had endings too; here we get only the first chapters of different novels, the titles of which themselves constitute a narrative:

> *If on a winter's night a traveler, outside the town of Malbork, leaning from the steep slope without fear of wind or vertigo, looks down in the gathering shadow in a network of lines that enlace, in a network of lines that intersect, on the carpet of leaves illuminated by the moon around an empty grave – What story down there awaits its end? – he asks, anxious to hear the story.*
>
> (258)

The inclusion of the title of Calvino's own novel at the start implicates the entire book in the general parody of narrative conventions, which (lest we miss them) are discussed one by one by the fictional readers in the library in chapter 11: "Do you believe that every story must have a beginning and an end? In ancient times a story could end only in two ways: having passed all the tests, the hero and the heroine married, or else they died" (259). Needless to say, that is how Calvino's novel ends or, rather, that is almost how it ends. The actual final words are those of the narrativized Reader to his wife, the Other Reader: "Just a moment, I've almost finished *If on a winter's night a traveler* by Italo Calvino" (260).

The reader required by this novel is clearly a fairly sophisticated one, although it is also true that, given the directive nature of the text, any reader would be bound to learn enough from the text itself to "get" some of the parodies, at least. The parodic echoes of Flann O'Brien or Borges or Nabokov may get missed, but many others are much more overt, and the didactic narrative voice is careful to ensure their comprehension: its manipulation of the reader does not end on that first page. There seems to be a difference in the degree of faith in reader competence between this novel and, say, Sterne's *Tristram Shandy*. In the eighteenth-century text, the narrator may indeed verbally manhandle his reader, but there still seems to be a tacit assumption that reader and narrator share a set of values and an educational background (so there is no need to translate foreign languages, for instance). There would seem to be little of this faith today, given the didacticism of much contemporary metafiction, such as John Fowles's *The French Lieutenant's Woman*. Critics have delighted for years now in pointing out the Victorian parodic elements in the text, the ironic echoes of Scott, George Eliot, Thackeray, Arnold, Dickens, Froude, and Hardy. But the modern narrator of this Victorian story dutifully points all of these out himself, along with references to Cervantes, Proust, Brecht, Ronsard, Flaubert, Milton, Radclyffe Hall, Catullus, Jane Austen, Arnold, Goethe, Dana, Tennyson, and Dickens. If literary games are being played with the reader of this novel, at least the rules of the game are being revealed very clearly.

Fowles has always worked in this open manner to instruct the reader of his novels. *The Collector* is overtly a double ironic parody of the fiction of Fowles's own generation of "angry young men" and of Shakespeare's *The Tempest*, and the characters' names are our first clue: "Ferdinand" Clegg (really Caliban) and Miranda. *The Magus* is more or less explicitly constructed upon the parodied forms of the *Bildungsroman*, the gothic tale, the masque, psycho-drama, and fantasy. It is in *The Ebony Tower* that the directness of the narrative voice of *The French Lieutenant's Woman* is replaced by a thematic allegory of the function of parody. In the title story, as we have already seen in an earlier chapter, an artist is perceived as using parody to buttress and deepen his painting: "beneath the modernity of so many of the surface elements there stood both a homage and a kind of thumbed nose to a very old tradition" (1974, 18). This is precisely the range of ethos that I have argued for all modern parody.

In writing a parody of the Victorian novel in *The French Lieutenant's Woman*, Fowles has created what Bakhtin called a "double-voiced" or hybrid form: it is not a pastiche or an imitation. And it is largely the modern narrator who prevents the monological trivialization of the imitative impulse. In a move similar to that of Post-Modernist architecture, Fowles suggests that out of earlier artistic modes can come new forms, forms that will teach the reader to read through the lenses of books. While retaining all the moral and social concerns of James and the English novel tradition, Fowles can offer something new. In the spate of interviews and articles that accompanied the commercial success of this novel, Fowles frequently compared his handling of parodic material to that of works now familiar to us: to Stravinsky's eighteenth-century reworkings, to the use of Velázquez made by Picasso and Bacon, to Prokofiev's "Classical" Symphony. But what is the function of this parody, beyond the manifesting of the virtuosity of the artist?

In this novel, the reader is clearly directed, even instructed, by the narrative voice (as in Calvino's novel) but also by the parodic structures themselves. Here parody has what we might even call an ideological function, for such rehandling of the conventions of the past functions in such a way as to direct the reader to the moral and social concerns of the novel. The simple theme of the changes over a century of social and literary evolution would not be very interesting, but Fowles is not claiming any modern superiority. He says that he is dealing with human constants, and that the only changes are those of vocabulary and metaphor. It is not the existence of this temporal telescoping, then, that is significant, but its function. This is the point at which parody takes on dimensions beyond the literary confines of the text, becoming a metaphor for broader contexts: the readers of this novel are never allowed to abstain from recognizing the parody or from judging and questioning themselves (by condemning the novel's world as Victorian and therefore as a thing of the past). They are forced to relate the past to the present – on the social and moral level, as well as on the literary one.

There is also a long tradition in parodic literature of placing readers in tricky positions and forcing them to make their own way. The rules, if the author is playing fair, are usually in the text itself. They may not be as overtly and didactically presented as in the works of Calvino and Fowles, but readers can infer some parodic intention once they have perceived the markers of the encoded presence of "double-directed" discourse. Claude Simon wrote his novel, *Triptyque* (1973), after seeing a Francis Bacon exhibit in Paris. Inspired by the painter's formal structuring of his art and his challenge to representation, Simon seems to have chosen to parody the related but novelistic conventions of description. The things described in this work, therefore, are made to change ontological identity through the text. The same object will be the subject of a first-level narrative, a painting, a poster, a film, and so on, but all recounted in a novel, of course. Near the end of the text a character completes a puzzle of the image with which the novel opens – an allegory of the complex and demanding act of interpretation and recognition of interdiscursive parody by the reader.

Much parodic metafiction today deliberately works either to orient or to disorient the reader. One of the effects of *both* kinds of maneuvering is to set up what one critic calls a "dialectical relationship between identification and distance which enlists the audience in contradiction" (Belsey 1980, 97). Like Brecht's *Verfremdungseffekt*, parody works to distance and, at the same time, to involve the reader in a participatory hermeneutic activity. Of course, there are many ways of accomplishing this – from aggression to seduction. In other words, being made to feel that we are actively participating in the generation of meaning is no guarantee of freedom; manipulators who make us feel in control are no less present for all their careful concealment. Some novelists even revel in this masquerading: Severo Sarduy, like many of the writers of the French *nouveau nouveau roman*, argues on the one hand for the expulsion of the author as the unique centre or omnipotent emitter of the text, but, on the other hand, he is happy to gloat over the hidden traps and "secret mechanisms" that he has encoded in his works – some for his friends, some only for himself (1972, 43). The most notorious of such authors is probably Jean Ricardou, whose critical output (see, for example, 1972) is largely devoted to explicating his own novels, novels which he insists are only the reader's task to interpret. Unfortunately, without the clues to the cryptogrammatic enigmas – clues provided by the author himself – such a task turns out to be almost impossible. Here the author is clearly trying to exercise a control, not only over the reader but over the reader as critic.

But how real is that control? Can any reader not choose to disregard such intentional statements, to disregard parodic references, for that matter? But would we still talk of parody? Like all codes (Eco 1979, 7), parodic codes, after all, have to be *shared* for parody – as parody – to be comprehended. Whether parody is intended as subversive of established canons or as a conservative force, whether it aims to praise or humble (Yunck 1963, 30) the original text, in either case the reader has to decode it *as parody* for the intention to be fully realized. Readers are active co-creators of the parodic text in a more explicit and perhaps more complex way than reader-response critics argue that they are in the reading of all texts. While all artistic communication can take place only by virtue of tacit contractual agreements between encoder and decoder, it is part of the particular strategy of both parody and irony that their acts of communication cannot be considered completed unless the precise encoding intention is realized in the recognition of the receiver. In other words, in addition to the usual artistic codes, readers must also recognize that what they are reading *is* a parody, and to what degree and of what type. They must also, of course, know the text or conventions being parodied, if the work is to be read as other than any piece of literature – that is, any non-parodic piece.

This is clear from a study conducted by psychologists (Miller and Bacon 1971) examining reaction to a *Harvard Lampoon* parody of *Playboy*, wherein the centrefold nude was presented with the suntanned/bikini-white areas of her body reversed. The investigators considered only two things, however, in determining the response of their subjects: their knowledge (from observation and experience) of tanning patterns, and the results of a psychological test measured on what is called the Rokeach Dogmatism Scale. The reason for this was their desire to study recognition of response to parodic humor in terms of open- and closed-mindedness. What they did not consider – but should have – was that their young student subjects might not have understood what parody as a genre was or that they might not have known the original *(Playboy)* code well enough to recognize the full humor, such as it is. In the optimal situation, the sophisticated subject would know the backgrounded work(s) well and would bring about a superimposition of texts by the mediation of that parodied work upon the act of viewing or reading. This act would parallel the parodist's own synthesis and would complete the circuit of meaning. It is this sharing of codes or coincidence of intention and recognition in parody, as well as in irony, that creates what Booth has called "amicable communities" (Booth 1974, 28) between encoders and decoders. The reader or viewer gets what one critic calls "an extra fillip" of pleasure from completing his or her part of the meaning circuit (Worchester 1940, 42). This, of course, also leaves both irony and parody open to accusations of elitism – the major point of attack against much metafiction today as well.

We have seen that, if readers miss a parodic allusion, they will merely read the text like any other: the pragmatic ethos would be neutralized by the refusal or inability to share the necessary mutual code that would permit the phenomenon to come into being. While "refusal" suggests will and intent, "inability" raises the issue of reader competence. It has been argued that irony requires of its reader a triple competence: linguistic, rhetorical or generic, and ideological (Kerbrat-Orecchioni 1980, 116). The basic need for linguistic competence is most evident in the case of irony, where the reader has to comprehend what is *implied,* as well as what is actually stated. Such linguistic sophistication would be assumed as a given by a genre like parody that employed irony as a rhetorical mechanism. The generic or rhetorical competence of the reader presupposes a knowledge of rhetorical and literary norms in order to permit the recognition of deviation from those norms that constitute the canon, the institutionalized heritage of language and literature. If the reader fails to recognize a parody as a parody (itself a canonical aesthetic convention) and as a parody of a certain work or set of norms (in whole or in part), then he or she will lack this competence. Perhaps it is for this reason that parody is a genre that, as we have seen, appears to flourish primarily in "democratically" culturally sophisticated societies. We should recall that little or no parodic material has been found in very early Hebrew and Egyptian literature, while it obviously flourished in Greece in the satyr plays and, most obviously, in the comedies of Aristophanes.

The third kind of competence is the most complex and can be called ideological in the broadest sense of the word. Parody is frequently accused of being an elitist form of discourse, largely because its pragmatic dimension implies that at least part of the locus of aesthetic value and meaning has been placed in the relation of reader to text – in other words, that parody exists potentially in "double-voiced" words (the result of textual superimposition) – but it is realized or actualized only by those readers who meet certain requisite conditions, such as ability or training. It is in this sense that there is an ideological as well as generic competence implied: in Todorov's (1978a, 291) terms, we are in the realm of the paradigmatic (not syntagmatic) context of the knowledge shared by the two locutors and also by the society to which they belong. The reader who does not "get" the parody is the one whose predicted expectations are somehow faulty. Parody, like irony, can therefore be said to require a certain institutionalized set of values – both aesthetic (generic) and social (ideological) – in order to be understood, or even to exist. The interpretive or hermeneutic situation is one based upon accepted norms, even if those norms only exist to be transgressed, as we saw in the last chapter.

In parodically encoding a text, producers must assume both a shared cultural and linguistic set of codes and the familiarity of the reader with the text parodied; if they do not, or suspect that they should not make that assumption, we find those overtly didactic texts of Calvino and Fowles. In Carmela Perri's (1978, 300) rewriting of John Searle's (1969, 94-6) illocutionary rules of reference to fit the act of alluding, the first rule is that the alluding author and his or her audience share the same language and cultural tradition. Since parody is a particular and complex form of ironic allusion, her subsequent listing of the stages of "perlocutionary effect" of alluding on the reader is also of interest to us. The reader is said to *comprehend* the literal (non-allusive or non-parodic) significance of what she calls the allusion-marker; she/he then *recognizes* it as an echo of a past source (either intra- or intertextual), *realizes* that "construal" is required, so then *remembers* aspects of the source text's "intension" which can then be *connected* to the alluding – or parodic – text in order to complete the marker's meaning (Perri 1978, 301). This description of the effects of a successfully performed allusion does not, however, take into account the response to the process itself: the pleasure of recognition, the delight in critical difference, or perhaps in the wit of such a superimposition of texts. It is interesting that in Bakhtin's many descriptions of the joyous carnival and its parodic modes there is little sense of wit and humor. One of the reasons for this lack is probably Bakhtin's utopian populism: it is as if he were determined to underplay those characteristics which might suggest ironic exclusivity or learnèd elitism.

   Although I mentioned earlier that we do not have a coherent way of dealing with textual production today that will satisfy the needs of a theory of parody, it is also true that critics of parodic – and difficult – avant-garde forms of art frequently choose what one of them calls a "phenomenological concentration upon the mental processes of the artist" (Butler 1980, 5). There is a return to Hirschian intention in order to explain the complexity of the texts being considered. From this perspective, Christopher Butler (1980, 115, 120-1) argues that, while all avant-garde forms are intended to be elitist by nature and therefore have traditionally been the province of the anti-bourgeois (at least in Europe), today's particular postmodernist modes are more eclectic, egalitarian, and accessible. Certainly parody demands of the (real and inferred) parodist much skill, craftsmanship, critical understanding, and, often, wit. He or she must be "encyclopedic, learnèd, obsessively cultured...burdened with the wastes of time, with cultural shards and rubbish" (Poirier 1968, 347). But the reader too must share a certain amount of this sophistication, if not skill, for it is the reader who must effect the decoding of the superimposed texts by means of his or her generic competence. This is not a matter (as in intertextuality) of a general ability to call upon what one has read, but, rather, it is specific to the particular text or conventions being parodied. For some artists, such a reliance upon the reader might be interpreted as functioning in an almost therapeutic way, as a kind of gambling on the success of an act of artistic exorcism (Kennedy 1980). The structural parodic act of incorporation and synthesis (whose strategy or function for the reader, we might recall, is paradoxically one of ironic contrast or separation) might be seen as the means for some writers to shake off stylistic influences, to master and so supersede an influential predecessor: one thinks of Proust's *L'Affaire Lemoine*. Parody would then be one more mode to add to Harold Bloom's catalog of ways in which modern writers cope with the "anxiety of influence" (Bloom 1973).

   Many traditional realistic novelists, for instance, seem to have begun or ended their careers by writing ironic parody: Jane Austen's major work opened with *Northanger Abbey* and Flaubert's ended with *Bouvard et Pécuchet*. This phenomenon suggests a need on the part of the artist to come to terms at some point in his or her career – even if only through irony – with formal literary conventions and with the past. Parody could be seen, then, as an act of emancipation: irony and parody can act to signal distance and control in the encoding act. Perhaps this is what Gide intended: his greatest parody of the novel form is paradoxically and ironically the only one of his works which he labeled a novel: *The*

Counterfeiters. In *As I Lay Dying* Faulkner was not only testing the technical limits of the novel genre; he was also coming to terms with the past of American literature. The passage in which Addie Bundren describes her affair with the Reverend Whitfield is a signal to the reader to see the dramatis personae of Hawthorne's *The Scarlet Letter* in modern ironic dress (or, here, undress): Addie is an unpunished Hester; Whitfield, as his name suggests, is her conveniently repentive Dimmesdale; their adulterous offspring is a Jewel, if not a Pearl. Addie's selfish cry that "My children were of me alone" has none of the noble integrity of Hester's refusal to name her lover and fellow sinner. Satire here mixes with parody to challenge modern moral perspectives, and the connection to the earlier classic and also the significant differences from it are the literary vehicles for the satiric attack.

In her book, *Poetic Artifice: A Theory of Twentieth-Century Poetry* (1978), Veronica Forrest-Thomson argues that the poet in our century acts as a mediator between the codes we normally recognize and use and those that emerge from an assimilation and transformation of those codes, or languages (xiv). Through parody, a link with the poetry of the past can be established, a link to an "accepted world of discourse" (81). In other words, a poet like Eliot can act as "tribal mediator," recalling the forms and values of the past without changing them; indeed, their value lies in their endurance, in their unchanging quality. Parody, especially of the reverential variety, becomes, then, a way to preserve continuity in discontinuity. The continuity is what we have called the conservative impulse of parody. But its opposite, the revolutionary drive argued by the Russian formalists, makes its appearance in the shape of the complexity which derives from the "double-voicing," from the parodic incorporation that leads to renewal through synthesis. In other words, the two impulses of parody that we studied separately in the last chapter can now be seen as operating in tandem in modernist verse, and, I would argue, also in postmodernist fiction.

It is also often possible to infer from a parodic text a certain vitalizing, competitive response on the part of the encoder to the past of his art. Doing consciously what time does more slowly, parody can work to distort the shapes of art, synthesizing from them and from the present of the encoder a new form – one not burdened, but enriched, by the past. In *Il male oscuro*, Giuseppe Berto presents a narrator-writer who seems, at first, to be functioning as would any narrator who was (within the story) a character involved in a psychoanalytic situation. It is only much later in the book that this narrator, as writer, self-consciously admits that everything he ever knew about analysis he learned from Italo

Svevo's novel, *The Confessions of Zeno*, and from Svevo's own comments. Berto's work adopts and adapts themes and structures from the earlier novel, but the narrator makes it clear that he realizes that he cannot repeat Svevo's work, even if he does share Zeno's problems (psychological and literary). In thematic terms, it is important that the narrator be "cured" of his "obscure malady" when he burns the first chapters of the very traditional novel he had written. At that point, Berto's novel too must end: the new parodic form has literally superseded the old and its work is now complete as well. Parody of such an extended sort as this cannot be said to be occasional. It is not like the short pieces in *Punch* or the *New Yorker*; it does not age any faster than other genres because it literally (and didactically) incorporates, and dialectically and ironically transcends, the literary past of the parodist.

This example, like that of the Fowles and Calvino novels we looked at earlier, is quite overt in its teaching of the reader, and as such is typical of much postmodernist writing. Modernist texts, however, do not usually appear so accommodating, as we have seen. The enigmatic and complex form of the work of Eliot, Pound, Yeats, or Mallarmé might suggest less of a direct concern to accommodate the reader. Or does it merely imply a greater confidence in reader competence than can be indulged in by writers today? Certainly Dante could assume more about his smaller readership and its position within a literary culture than could, say, Donne, and Donne in turn could assume more than Eliot. But maybe Eliot could assume more than a novelist like Fowles today dares to. Perhaps our present culture, for all its global-village aspects, does lack that cohesion and stability which Herman Meyer lamented (1968, 20). It is too easy to turn to the clichés of Eliot's royalism or Pound's fascism in order to assert their elitism, their conservative nostalgia for a social and cultural set of norms. But one could just as easily argue that the process of reading *The Waste Land*, of having to recall (or learn) the works of the past alluded to in the poem, is in itself the way in which the situation of the "waste land" of our civilization will be remedied. Eliot's serious, reverential parody of his literary and cultural heritage – presented in such a new and unfamiliar form for most of his contemporary readers – could be seen to mark his ultimate trust in the reader: a trust, if not in his or her present competence, at least in the willingness to work towards achieving such breadth and depth of culture as to make the comprehension of the text possible. Such is one way of inferring the intentionality of that poem, one that complicates this issue considerably, since elitism can be seen to suggest less a lack of democratic egalitarianism than the faith in a capacity to learn, in an openness to the teachings of art, be they overt or covert. Like Joyce and Mann, Eliot could be said to use parody in order to capitalize on its doubleness, "to harmonize within art the corresponding schisms within the culture" (Kiremidjian 1969, 242). Like them, he may be seen to work toward the continuing of a cultural tradition that would guarantee a certain community of cultural horizons, that would act as a "stay against the slippage of centers of belief" (Benamou 1977, 4). In postmodernist art, this co-opting function of parody may change, but its form remains to activate in the reader or viewer that collective participation that enables something closer to active "performance" to replace the "well-wrought urn" of modernist closure.

As we saw in the last chapter, we must be careful not to equate automatically words like transgression with positive revolutionary change; nor, however, must we assume that elitism is necessarily a negative term. The ideological status of parody cannot be permanently fixed and defined: "Parody, or 'reflexive art,' like this where signifiers refer to other previous signifiers in a formal game of inter-textuality has no necessary relationship to radical innovation at either a formal, avant-garde level or a political, vanguard level" (Nichols 1981, 65). Nor, however, does it necessarily imply any undemocratic and negative notion of elitism. Is there really a contradiction between Edward Bond's radical socialism and his "encouraging elitism" (Rabinowitz 1980, 263) in the Shakespearian references in *Lear*? Parody's sharing of codes can be used to many different ends; in each case the inferred intent must be determined individually. There is no doubt that parody, like allusion and quotation, can act as a kind of "badge of learning" for both encoders and decoders (Morawski 1970, 690), that it can work toward maintaining cultural continuity. But one could also argue, as did the Russian formalists, that, in so doing, parody makes possible change – even radical change.

6

CONCLUSION: THE WORLD, THE PARODIC TEXT, AND THE THEORIST

It is the loss of memory, not the cult of memory, that will make us prisoners of the past.   *Paolo Portoghesi*

The title of this chapter is obviously a (parodic) reworking of that of Edward Said's *The World, the Text, and the Critic* (1983). In that book, Said argues for a literary theory that would take account of what he calls "the text's situation in the world" (151). Given his belief that all art is discourse-specific – that is, that it cannot escape its historical, social, and ideological context – his position is that all texts, even parodic ones, are "worldly, to some degree that they are events, and, even when they appear to deny it [as in self-reflexive parodic texts], they are nevertheless a part of the social world, human life, and of course, the historical moments in which they are located and interpreted" (4). This chapter is an attempt to do what Said asks of critics and theorists: "to read and write with a sense of the greater stake in historical and political effectiveness that literary as well as other texts have had" (225). To do this, it is hoped, is to work towards a de-marginalization of literature – and of theory.

In the last five chapters, the "worldly" or ideological status of parody has been touched on a number of times. Much parody, we saw, turned out to be conservative or normative in its critical function. This is especially true of the ridiculing kind that is usually the only kind permitted to be called parody. According to a Romantic aesthetic, such forms of art are by definition parasitic. Even today, this same negative evaluation persists and its basis, as betrayed by its language, is often ideological in a very general sense: we are told that parody seeks to dominate texts, but that it is still ultimately peripheral and parasitic (Stierle 1983, 19-20).

We have also seen, however, that there is another kind of parody, different from the traditional mocking type that is often both limited in size and text-specific (or occasional). This other kind or mode has a wider range of pragmatic ethos and its form is considerably more extended. Parody in much twentieth-century art is a major mode of thematic and formal structuring, involving what I earlier called integrating modeling processes. As such, it is one of the most frequent forms taken by textual self-reflexivity in our century. It marks the intersection of creation and re-creation, of invention and critique. Parody "is to be understood as a mode of aesthetic foregrounding in the novel. It defines a particular form of historical consciousness, whereby form is created to interrogate itself against significant precedents; it is a serious mode" (Burden 1979, 136). It is this "historical consciousness" of parody that gives it the potential power both to bury the dead, so to speak, and also to give it new life (Bethea and Davydov 1981, 8).

Parody is, then, an important way for modern artists to come to terms with the past – through ironic recoding or, in my awkward descriptive neologism, "trans-contextualizing." Its historical antecedents are the classical and Renaissance practices of imitation, though with more stress on difference and distance from the original text or set of conventions. Since I have defined present-day parody as repetition with difference, I have inevitably placed it within an entire post-structuralist debate on the nature of repetition. In Chapter 4 I argued that parody presupposes both a law and its transgression, or both repetition and difference, and that therein lies the key to its double potential: it can be both conservative and transformative, both "mystificatory" (Rosler 1983, 204) and critical. Such a view fits into neither of the two camps in the contemporary debate (see Cobley 1984). Parody is not repetition that stresses sameness and stasis; it is not seen primarily as a stabilizing agent that can unify or emphasize (Kawin 1972). Nor, however, is parody simply a post-structuralist differential or relational kind of repetition that stresses only difference. Parody certainly can be disruptive and destabilizing; it is as such that the Russian formalists gave it its major role in the evolution of literary forms. According to Gilles Deleuze, repetition is always by nature transgression, exception, singularity (1968, 12). Yet parody, while often subversive, can also be conservative; in fact, parody is by nature, paradoxically, an authorized transgression. It cannot be accounted for only in terms of *différance*, deferral, even if it is true today that, for many artists and theorists, a stress on undecidability has replaced previous concerns for aesthetic unity, even in diversity (Derrida 1978; 1968, 46, 51, 57). Parody is both textual doubling (which unifies and reconciles) and differentiation (which foregrounds irreconcilable opposition between texts and between text and "world").

An overtly "worldly" example will perhaps make this paradox clearer. Karlheinz Stockhausen's *Hymnen: Anthems for Electronic and Concrete Sounds* uses well-known national anthems because his listeners, familiar with them, will then more easily be able to hear *how* they are reworked. But he also uses anthems because they are "loaded" with time and history. On the sleeve notes (Deutsche Grammophon Gesellschaft 2707 039) Stockhausen explains his intention to repeat in order to unify and integrate the old and familiar with the new (noises from crowds, short-wave radios, speeches, and various electronic sounds). Yet the listener, as the composer is aware, is just as struck by the separation, the isolation – the difference, in short – as he or she is by the intermodulation of fragments. In parodic repetition, if not in all repetition (Rimmon-Kenan 1980, 152), difference is a necessary defining characteristic; but sameness is not, for all that, merely obliterated. Parody manages to inscribe continuity while permitting critical distance and change.

Throughout this study, my way of approaching a theory of parody has been to start in the same way with the ubiquity and importance of modern parody (in a variety of art forms) and, from there, to work toward the formulation of a theory that would account for the kind of complex phenomenon modern parody is. We need only think of a work like Lukas Foss's *Baroque Variations* to see this complexity. The entire piece of music is a kind of gloss on Bach, a commentary both on our view of the past tradition, which is the unavoidable and unchanging source of many musical ideas, and also on our experience of the present, the individuality of each performance. One section is called "Phorion," meaning "stolen goods." Like Brecht playing reverently, but not slavishly, with Shakespeare, Foss shows both his respect for and willingness to rework the music of cult figures. The composer himself calls it a "particular act of love-violence." Foss's remarks on the sleeve of the Nonesuch recording (H-71202) explain that he uses the notes of the original texts, but then fragments and deletes them. The first variation is what he calls "perforated Handel!" (Concerto Grosso, Op. 6, No. 12). In the second, a play on Scarlatti's Sonata No. 23, the background harpsichord plays the entire piece, while the foreground fragments it. According to Foss, it is "an abuse, an homage." Only the "Phorion" section (which parodies Bach's Partita in E Major for solo violin) adds some traditional parodic jokes, as a xylophone spells out Johann Sebastian Bach's name in Morse code.

To deal with this complex and extended kind of parody in terms of the "world" as well as in aesthetic terms, we have found that we need to go beyond those reductive dictionary definitions of parody in two important ways. First, we must reconsider the nature and direction of the so-called "target" of parody. The parodied text today is often not at all under attack. It is often respected and used as a model – in other than artistic ways. For example, the recent film, *Carney*, is a parody of the famous movie *Freaks*; in fact, it is a Bakhtinian carnivalesque inversion of a film which is itself a carnivalesque inversion. The young blonde woman in *Carney* is basically a positive character, even if she does prove to be a rival in the friendship between two men. The inversion of the original here consists in the fact that the blonde woman in *Freaks* is a negative character, a rival in the love of the two dwarfs, one male and one female. The modern film is about male bonding, rather than about heterosexual love, itself somewhat inverted in *Freaks* by the seeming "travesty" affair between the dwarf male and the large, normal woman. In both films there is a ritualistic mutilation, although in the new version it turns out to be an illusion. In both cases, however, the blonde woman turns out to belong to the carnival world, though for different reasons. In *Freaks* she is literally made into a mutilated carnival freak; of course, the film makes clear that it is she, not the various dwarfs and other physically deformed performers, who is the real freak, the real social misfit, the truly evil character to be feared. In *Carney*, a police officer announces that today's carnivals cannot show freaks any more; but normal people proceed to take on their function. Here the blonde woman belongs to the carnival world because she learns its ethic. She is, as the difference in the titles makes clear, a *carney* and not a *freak*.

The need to reconsider the "target" of parody involves a second move away from the standard definitions of parody: we must open up the range of pragmatic ethos or intended responses of parody. In doing so, we must consider the role of irony, as we did in Chapters 2 and 3. To consider in this way both the inferred production and the actual reception of parodic texts is to allow for the consideration of the "text's situation in the world." There is, in fact, a recent trend in German parody criticism to see parody as *Ideologiekritik* (Karrer 1977; Rose 1979; Freund 1981) which either can be used at the expense of the original text's ideology or can hold that ideology up as an ethical standard (Freund 1977). From this point of view, parody acts as a consciousness-raising device, preventing the acceptance of the narrow, doctrinaire, dogmatic views of any particular ideological group. However, as many more "conservative" parodists have proved, this need not be the case. What is needed in such theory is a clearer notion of the differences between and interaction of parody and satire, as well as more of an awareness of the paradoxical status of parody's ideology as authorized transgression.

To offer a theory of parody that is pragmatic as well as formalist is to suggest, then, that there is a "worldly" connection on at least two separate levels: on that of the relation of parody to satire, and on that of the need to consider the entire enunciative act in any consideration of parody. The lesson of much parody theory today is that we must be very careful to separate parody from satire. Some of the most interesting work on parody is, in the end, made confused, not to say muddled, by the lack of such a distinction (Morson 1981; Rose 1979). In Chapters 2 and 3 we saw that the interaction of parody and satire is a complex one, but it is not a confused or confusing one, given their different "targets" (intra- and extramural) and their different affinities with the rhetorical trope most common to both: irony.

Satire is certainly one of the ways of bringing the "world" into art, and parodic satire and satiric parody enable parody too to be "worldly," if in a very obvious way. The work of Bertolt Brecht has perhaps been the best modern model for the use of parody to satiric ends (Weisstein 1970-1) and has undoubtedly had an important influence on the popularity of parody in modern German literature (Freund 1981, 95, 105). Brecht was not just an ideologue; he was also a master parodist who could use parody to make the entire issue of theatrical representation implode (Pfrimmer 1971, 75). His *Threepenny Opera* (Brecht 1979) ends with a thematized parody of the standard operatic ending: "Since this is opera, not life, you'll see / Justice give way before humanity. / So now, to stop our story in its course / Enter the royal official on his horse" (2, ii, 78). And, of course, Brown does duly enter with Macheath's reprieve and even a peerage from the Queen. Kurt Weill claimed, however, that this was not parody in the traditional mocking sense of the word. It was, rather, "an instance of the very idea of 'opera' being used to resolve a conflict, i.e. being given a function in establishing the plot" (99). Brecht also transposes the time period of Gay's original work to the bourgeois Victorian times in which grand opera and capitalism went hand in hand. But what Handel was to Gay, Wagner is to Brecht and Weill. The modern music jars with the Victorian setting, just as the beggars who want to portray Victorian respectability often lapse into vulgarity, especially in their songs, and the grand manner collapses. In *Arturo Ui* Brecht used parody as a mode of distanciation to create the epic theatre's critical attitude. It destroys the psychological motivation by which the audience might explain away the brutal reality of corruption and violence that must, instead, be faced (Pfrimmer 1971, 83).

In the work of Brecht, parody and satire interact in a complex and particularly effective way. In contemporary fiction too, parody permits the critical distance that can engender contact with the "world," again often through satire. In Angus Wilson's *No Laughing Matter*, the parodies both of the dynastic family saga à la Galsworthy and of the conventions of dramatic language (as being close to the language of social interaction) undermine (while imitating) the conventions of realism. There is in the novel the suggestion that the formal dislocations are meant to mirror the disintegration of the social world in which those conventions were rooted (Burden 1979, 137). This kind of satiric parody can also function in less extended forms. In David Lodge's self-consciously parodic novel, *The British Museum is Falling Down*, the hero, working in the British Museum in Bloomsbury, notes: "From nearby Westminster, Mrs Dalloway's clock boomed the half hour. It partook, he thought, shifting his weight in the saddle, of metempsychosis, the way his humble life fell into moulds prepared by literature" (1965, 37). The parody of Virginia Woolf's style and of her technique of mingling the trivial and the significant to create psychological realism is clever, for we cannot help recalling the dinner party in *To the Lighthouse* at which Mrs Ramsay serves her sacramental *bœuf en daube*: "It partook, she felt, carefully helping Mr Bankes to a specially tender piece, of eternity." If we make that connection, though, we also recall that that epiphanic communion was attended by the sterile academic Charles Tansley, who is finally revealed to be inadequate, as indeed may the otherwise fertile hero of Lodge's novel. On a larger scale, it is the "worldly" values of Bloomsbury, as well as its style, that are being recalled. The British Museum may be falling down, but the disintegration of what it represents is lamented and not ridiculed. This is the same kind of satiric parody that we find in Fowles's *The French Lieutenant's Woman* or, more recently, in another novel that parodies the Victorian novel in order to reveal what the Victorian world hid: Joyce Carol Oates's *A Bloodsmoor Romance*. This work has been called "revisionist melodrama" (Mars-Jones 1983, 79) in its parody of the novel form's refusal to be more open and its satire of the society that did the same.

In some ways, though, this mixing of parody and satire is not new to the novel. Readers of the works of Samuel Richardson were used to the convention of using asterisks instead of names, presumably in order to preserve anonymity. In the hands of Sterne, in *Tristram Shandy*, the use of the asterisks can become redundant, for he provides us with enough information to identify easily the person or place. Or he might use them as a means of censoring or creating suspense. Often the practice seems so arbitrary that Tristram appears to be using the little stars to avoid bothering to write the speech. Usually, however, the omissions are suggestive – sexually suggestive. It is, perhaps, the underlying prurience of Richardson's reticence that is being satirized through Sterne's parody of the convention.

This parody/satire interaction is not, then, new to the novel; nor is it unique to literature. The bicentennial year in the United States inspired a spate of parodies of patriotic paintings such as Gilbert Stuart's portrait of George Washington, or Trumbull's *The Battle of Bunker's Hill* and *Signing the Declaration of Independence*. The title of Larry Rivers's *An Outline of History* parodies one American institution, while the painting itself is literally just an outline of Trumbull's *Signing*. And among the signatures is that of Bob Morris, a notoriously independent artist. Ad Reinhardt's satires of the fifties' art scene in New York took parodic form, but their "worldly" connection was clear: he wanted to stop painters from selling the art world out for money (Hess 1974, 51). Jasper Johns's *White Flag* painting satirizes America's cult of its flag. In it we find parodied the familiar stars and stripes on cloth, but this flag is fixed and flat, and cannot wave in the air. It has also been bleached of its evocative colours. Johns voids the flag's form of its emotional impact; he "abstracts" it into a painting (Hughes 1980, 340-1). In so doing, he makes us aware that flags are, in a sense, only abstract forms upon which social usage has conferred meaning. Johns's parody makes them cease to function socially.

There is a similar level of satiric comment in the films of Brian De Palma. *Dressed to Kill* is a parody of Hitchcock's *Psycho*, but the psycho or killer is, significantly, the psychiatrist. *Blowout*, as its title suggests, transposes the visual code of Antonioni's *Blow-Up* into an aural one, with the same political focus. The film opens with a deliberately bad parody of Hitchcock's *Psycho* which acts as a signal, as does the title, for the audience to look for parodic backgrounded texts. Within the bad parody, a woman's scream is so silly that it has to be re-recorded; within the film itself, the final scream of real pain is silent. In the end, the political dimension cannot be separated from the aesthetic, parodic one in this movie.

Satire, however, is not the only way in which the "world" can be seen to impinge on parody, as we have noted. There are at least two other, less obvious, levels of "worldliness" in parody, one rooted in the bi-directionality of the legitimacy of parody (Chapter 4) and the other based on the sharing of parodic codes (Chapter 5). The ideological status of parody is paradoxical, for parody presupposes both authority and its transgression, or, as we have just seen, repetition and difference. The implications of this paradox for the visual arts have been examined by Benjamin Buchloh (1982). He argues that Picabia's parodistic appropriation of the drawing style of engineering plans and diagrams is ultimately conservative: it only makes the linear, individual artist's drawings *appear* to be the blueprint of an anonymous technologist. In other words, while seeming to contest what I have called the Romantic aesthetic, this work does not really cancel out the artist's presence at all, or at least not in the same way that Duchamp's urinal does. In its challenge to the validity of the entire system of art, the latter replaces an individually crafted simulacrum with a real mass-produced object in actual space (Buchloh 1982, 30). Buchloh argues that parody can be both a mode of ultimate complicity and secret reconciliation and also a real way to revolutionize art. He points to Sigmar Polke and Gerhard Richter as German painters of the 1960s who used parody, as did American pop artists, to confront history and technology, combining an ironic appropriation from low-cultural forms with a stylistic appropriation from high art, juxtaposing "reified code and subversive codification" (33).

While acknowledging that parody often acts as a conservative authorizing of tradition, Buchloh also admits that it has the potential to "deny the validity of art practice as individuation" (34). By this he means more than parody's challenge to the Romantic aesthetic and even to the concept of the "subject"; he also intends to link appropriation or parody to a challenge to the capitalist view of art as individuality and therefore as private property. After all, the Latin root of the word appropriation is *proprium*, property – that which belongs to one person. Yet, while it is true that parodic borrowing or stealing challenges this, and that parody can certainly appropriate the past in order to effect a cultural critique, it is also true that any concept of textual appropriation must implicitly place a certain value upon the original. In fact, some have argued that the past is often pirated by the avant-garde as a way of both softening and giving meaning to radicalness: the new can shock only when underwritten by the old. Would Arnulf Rainer's altered photographs of his own distorted face have any meaning or impact without the long tradition of self-portraiture that goes back through the expressionistically heightened self-images of van Gogh and Kokoschka to their forerunners in Rembrandt and so many others (Hughes 1980, 253-4)? What I earlier called parody's authorized transgression could also be seen as a "conventional non-conventionality," "a possession *of* history in order to ensure one's place *in* history" (Barber 1983-4, 32).

A second way in which parody manifests its "worldliness" is that examined in Chapter 5. In arguing that any theory of parody must be based in a consideration of the entire act of the *énonciation* (the contextualized production and reception of texts), I wanted to stress that the "text's situation in the world" involved the sharing of codes in an act of communication between encoder and decoder. Jonathan Culler reveals an interest only in the latter (and only in a limited definition of parody) when he asserts: "In calling something a parody we are specifying how it should be read, freeing ourselves from the demands of poetic seriousness, and making curious features of the parody intelligible" (1975, 152). Parody, by this definition, becomes an ultimate act of co-opting, a making sense of the unintelligible by the imposition of the code of parody. This stress on the importance of the interpretive act of the receiver of the text has been reinforced by postmodernist views of parody as performance, as involving an increase in the work and participation of the decoder, forced to draw extensively on his or her artistic memory. But it is ideologically naïve, I think, to assert that such participation is necessarily more democratic, as does John Sturrock (1979, 17). As we saw in Chapter 5, the power of the aesthetic manipulation of the receiver exists; it is just a question of how aware we are made of it, or of how free we can be made to feel.

David Caute (1972) has argued that, if art wishes to make us question what I have been calling the "world," it must question and expose *itself* in the name of public action. It must become, in his terms, "dialectical" (33) and must focus, in literature, on both the writer and the reader (145), as must criticism that deals with it. I would argue that we must go one step further. We must take into account the entire enunciative act: the text and the "subject positions" of encoder and decoder, but also the various contexts (historical, social, ideological) that mediate that communicative act. Romanticism focused almost exclusively on the author; in reaction, formalism looked to the text; reader-response theory considers only the text and the reader. Parody today points to the need to go beyond these limitations. To repeat, even with critical difference, is to be part of that contemporary post-structuralist challenge to the notion of the subject as individual source of meaning. Composers like George Rochberg consciously work to subvert that ideology of the ego and personal style often associated historically with capitalism (see the sleeve notes to his String Quartet No. 3, Nonesuch H-71283). Literary parody also participates in the modern structuralist contesting of the notion of linguistic transparency. If texts refer to other texts, the entire notion of reference must be re-examined.

The third contemporary debate that touches on parody in a direct manner is that involving the questioning of the concepts of objectivity and closure. Metafiction today subverts formalist notions of closure by its self-referential reveling in parodic arbitrariness. In music today, parody has offered a way out of modernist closure, again through self-reflexivity. In the face of the isolation caused by the loss of a shared musical syntax, composers often turn to establish explicit links with older musical traditions which offer "a kind of historical resonance" (Morgan 1977, 46). George Crumb, for instance, invokes both medieval and nineteenth-century music through allusion; Penderecki's vocal compositions use chant-*like* materials. For these composers, the meaning of musical tradition has been changed by parody: "Instead of being something passed down in a continuous evolution from generation to generation, tradition itself becomes 'contextual.' Like the musical system, it is defined for each individual composition, which acquires its own unique historical correspondences" (Morgan 1977, 46). It is, in other words, the enunciative context of parody that changes artistic history and its meaning. These composers have also shown the need to modify the entire notion of context to include even ideological considerations. Adorno's work on the sociology of music is often cited as offering a way to destroy the isolation and closure of Western music, to prevent solipsism, despite both the loss of shared language and the necessary individuality of structures.

Paradoxically, perhaps, it is parody that implies this need to "situate" art in both the act of the *énonciation* and the broader historical and ideological contexts implied by that act. In literary criticism, it is exactly this dimension that had been banned by the earlier New Criticism (see Lentricchia 1980) and again by present-day formalist, phenomenological, hermeneutic, and post-structuralist theories (see Eagleton 1983). This would suggest that a theory of modern parody, therefore, must go beyond these particular orthodoxies, in the sense that it must not begin within any of these perspectives if it hopes to account for the paradoxical complexity of parody. Parody is not the archetypal example of formalist closure or of textual introversion that many have tried to make of it. It was Bakhtin, the valorizer of parody, who also argued that "The sign cannot be separated from the social situation without relinquishing its nature as sign" ([Bakhtin] Vološinov 1973, 95). Another thing that parody is *not* is an infinitely expandable modern paradigm of fictionality or textuality. The "world" may be more the site of textual forces than Said allows, but twentieth-century parodic practice does not really seem to license a Nietzschean extension of parody to what ultimately becomes a world-system (see Gilman 1976, 21-8).

Parody historicizes by placing art within the history of art; its inclusion

of the entire enunciative act and its paradoxical authorized transgression of norms allow for certain ideological considerations. Its interaction
with satire overtly makes room for added social dimensions. Woody
Allen's *Zelig* is a parody of an earlier film *They Might Be Giants,* complete with a male patient with a mania (he thinks he is Sherlock Holmes)
and a female psychiatrist (Dr Watson, of course). It is also, and more
significantly, a parody of the television and movie documentary form,
which makes its fictional hero the focus of his age, inserting him into
real historical scenes and commenting on his historical importance
through the words of real people (Susan Sontag, Saul Bellow, Irving
Howe). The story of the man who changed physically (nationality, race,
size) in order to be loved, in order to fit in, intersects with the rise of
Hitler and the horrific demise of those who did not fit in. The interaction
of parody and satire here is almost Brechtian in its ideological
effectiveness.

Parody also implies, though, another kind of "worldly" connection.
Its appropriating of the past, of history, its questioning of the contemporary by "referencing" it to a different set of codes, is a way of
establishing continuity that may, in itself, have ideological implications.
The corollary to modernism's aesthetic of autonomy and formalism was
its isolation from sociopolitical practice (Buchloh 1982, 28). Through
its found objects and its technological procedures of mechanical reproduction, Warhol and Rauschenberg's parodic pop art suggests an attack on
high-art discourse and its isolation from social reality. (This is not to
say that our capitalist culture is not capable of co-opting even these
challenges, making them into individual high-art productions and expensive private property.) In Benjamin Buchloh's somewhat awkward
terms:

> Parodistic appropriation reveals the split situation of the individual in con-
> temporary artistic practice. The individual must claim the constitution of
> the self in original primary utterances, while being painfully aware of the
> degree of determination necessary to inscribe the utterance into dominant
> conventions and rules of codification; reigning signifying practice must be
> subverted and its deconstruction placed in a distribution system (the market),
> a circulation form (the commodity), and a cultural legitimization system (the
> institutions of art). (1982, 30)

In present-day literature too, it is the "elitist" aestheticism associated
with modernism that is often the focus of parody that intends ideological
comment. In the first chapter we saw that Ezra Pound's Hugh Selwyn
Mauberley existed in a Dantesque hell, an ironic inversion of the aesthetic

and moral world of the *Divine Comedy*. Timothy Findley's subsequent use of Pound's text as the parodic background of his novel, *Famous Last Words*, adds another level of complexity to the ideological function of parody. Pound's anti-hero's "obscure reveries / of the inward gaze" are associated with destruction in the poem, but in Findley's novel Mauberley literally dies with an ice pick in the eye. Pound's soldiers, walking "eye-deep in hell" in death camps that outdo the "hysterias, trench confessions, / laughter out of dead bellies" of the war, reappear in Findley's novel to be witness to the confession of the one who ignored that horror in the name of beauty. The impotent love in Pound's poem (parodying Dante's chaste devotion to Beatrice) is again inverted in the novel in the fictional Mauberley's relationship with the historically real the Duchess of Windsor. We cannot separate parody and history in this novel; nor can we ignore the ideological commentary on the silence of aestheticism.

Literature, film, the visual arts, and music all can use parody today to comment on the "world" in some way. The art form that has most overtly and most programmatically appropriated the past to ideological ends, however, is clearly architecture, which is, in a sense, the most public of the arts. In so doing, it partakes in a general postmodernist desire to establish a dialogue with the past (Kristeva 1980b; Calinescu 1980). In poetry, this dialogue took the form of experiments with preformed linguistic texts "to find out whether it was possible to arrive at the new and significant through the use of the old and the trivial" (Antin 1980, 131). Like the composers, painters, novelists, and poets, architects too sought to give altered significances to previous works by parody which reframes or "trans-contextualizes" the past. What are known today by the label of Post-Modernist architects are an eclectic grouping who share a historical sense and a desire to return to architecture a sense of both communication and community. Their precursor in this latter aim is perhaps the Amsterdam school of architecture of the 1915-30 period (Piet Kramer, Michel de Klerk), which wanted to restore to the twentieth century, through architecture, the community spirit of the Middle Ages. (They did not choose to copy or parody medieval forms, however.)

Paolo Portoghesi is not alone among Post-Modernist architects in his strong emphasis on the importance of community and function (1974, viii). All see architecture as a humanizing force, one that parodies the past to ideological ends. But the past cannot help but be important for an architect working in Rome, faced not only with the layers of history but with the example of the baroque architects' means of dealing with that past. For Portoghesi, this parodic historical consciousness is the source of continuity – both aesthetic and social. He sees Post-Modernism as based in the interaction between historical memory and the new; in other words, it reveals the need to "trans-contextualize," to give buildings a new relation to both the past and to their present environment (1982, 29).

Charles Jencks and Paolo Portoghesi are the major theorists and spokesmen of architectural Post-Modernism. It is Jencks who has argued that architecture should be viewed as conveying meaning through language and convention, and that, therefore, we should look to the past to enlarge the vocabulary of form available to us. Our discourse with the past, he claims, is not in an integrated language like that of the Renaissance or baroque; instead, it is pluralistic and eclectic (1980a, 16). But it is definitely doubly coded or (in my terms here) parodic. The aim of Post-Modernist architecture, Jencks claims, is to

> supply a public discourse worthy of our time, an articulate and dignified speech which not only makes us see our past in a new and refreshing way, but also tells us coherently about the variety of different beliefs, ways of life and building functions. (16)

Aesthetic appropriation of the past, then, is motivated here by a reaction against the reductive and destructive influence of High Modernism on our urban environment. The consequences of Modernism are epitomized, for Jencks, by the contempt for place and function of the Pruitt–Igoe housing project in St Louis. Its literal destruction marked the failure of the Modernist ideology that pure aesthetic form would necessarily lead to proper social conduct (1977, 9).

For Portoghesi too, the enemy is Modernism, but he is also aware of the architect's Oedipal relationship to his immediate past – his need to break from it, but his temptation too to draw from it the primary materials of future construction (Portoghesi 1982, 3). Hence the use of parody, the double-coding of Post-Modernism. Modernism consciously and deliberately cut architecture off from its past; it was both elitist and obscure. In Portoghesi's analysis, Modernism is said to have survived as long as it has (and to have been as pervasive as it has been) because of the support provided by its alliance with power, with the industrial system (1982, 3). Jencks too links Modernism with monopolies and big business, with international exhibitions that fostered mass standards of acceptability, with those megabuildings that replaced factories and stores – the industrial complexes and shopping centers that Modernist architects built by the score (1977, 26-37). The new feats of engineering made possible by technology led to what many see as Modernism's fetishizing of the means of production – in terms of both technology and building materials. In so doing, Modernism *had* to reject historicism and the experience of the past in order to impose its analytic, geometric, rationalist aesthetic (and ideology) (Portoghesi 1982, 4). This disregard for collective memory interrupted the continuous process of the recycling of the past that constituted the creative transformation of all architecture (17).

This rejection of history had an overtly ideological component: architecture became an important part of the modern myth of social reform. The Modernist elitist rejection of all but pure form was presumed to have good social effects. That this was not, in fact, the case has been ably documented by Jane Jacobs in *The Death and Life of Great American Cities* (1961). Yet Modernism saw itself as "prophetic, severe, and prescriptive" (Portoghesi 1982, 29), utopian in its belief that architecture could shape the social behavior of the masses, especially through corporate structures or what Jencks (1982, 50) dubbed "Slick-Tech" or "Corporate Efficiency." The architect was the doctor or savior of society. Later, in the exaggeration of the tendencies of Modernism that Jencks labels as "Late-Modernism," the architect became a provider of service, with the suggestion of something egalitarian and agnostic in the concrete, steel, and glass fabrication.

Post-Modernism marks a conscious rejection of this ideology. Now the architect is seen more as an activist or a representative. But the fact that Post-Modern form is always, by definition, doubly coded ensures that Modernism is not rejected outright: it is critically reviewed, selectively parodied. This kind of architecture is, in fact, doubly parodic: it is a reworking of modernism *and* of some other tradition as well. In public buildings, where ideology is most visible, perhaps, the other tradition parodied is often that of classical architecture. The reason for this is given by architect Robert Stern:

> In the search for a wider base for form, the classical tradition offers a set of references that remain meaningful to the public and continue to demonstrate their compositional usefulness to architects. In recognizing this, we do not necessarily argue for a return to or revival of the past, but rather for a recognition of the continuity of the past in the present. (Cited in Jencks 1980b, 35)

Even in private housing, architects sought to add a public dimension by fusing local domestic styles with classicism: Thomas Gordon Smith's Matthews St House Project and his Tuscan and Laurentian Houses are good examples of this kind of double parody. This is not just an elitist quoting or resemanticizing of previous architectural languages. Even Modernists did that, especially in those homes they designed for consumer magazine photos (Jencks and Chaitkin 1982, 74, 77, 83). This is also not straight revivalism, as in Quinlan Terry's upper-class English country houses. There is a necessary ironic distance involved here in being the custodian of the architectural legacy. In its absorption of conflicting codes, Post-Modernism is pluralistic and ironic. This can be seen in the double significance of its use of ornament. Any use of ornament is immediately anti-Modernist; yet Charles Moore's columns and fountains in his Piazza d'Italia, for all their classical ornamentation, are prefab. They are not hand-crafted decoration; Romantic individuality and Gothic craftsmanship have been replaced by Modernist machine-tooled impersonality. But this is all set in the context of a celebration of public identity (that of the Italian community of New Orleans). The Oedipal complex of the architect towards his Modernist past is clear.

Architectural parody, in this sense, has ideological implications because, as Jencks (Jencks and Chaitkin 1982, 178) argues, it both *is* and *represents*. It marks a return not only to the past, but, simultaneously, to what the past stood for, to both function and communication. It is not surprising that many Post-Modernists see their precursor as being Edwin Lutyens, the anti-Modernist contemporary of Frank Lloyd Wright, whose stylistic parodies of historical and contemporary sources were put to the use and desire of those who would actually inhabit his creations.

The return to function and communication is what allows the element of ideology to enter Post-Modernist architectural parody. In their work on Las Vegas, the Venturis, according to Jencks,

> want to express, in a gentle way, a mixed appreciation for the American Way of Life. Grudging respect, not total acceptance. They don't share all the values of a consumer society, but they want to speak to this society, even if partially in dissent. (1977, 70)

Post-Modern architecture reveals everything from a Fowlesian irreverent "thumbed nose" to a "homage" to the past, both the aesthetic and the social past. But, like all modern parody, it always does so through repetition with critical difference. Again it is Robert Stern who best expresses this:

> Our attitude toward form, which is based in a love for history and an awareness of it, does not imply accurate reproduction. It is eclectic and is used as a technique of collage and juxtaposition, to give new meaning to known forms and thereby goes off in new directions. Our faith is in the power of memory (history), combined with richness and meaning. If architecture is to succeed in its attempt to creatively participate in the present, it is necessary that it overcome the iconoclasm of the last fifty years of the modern movement or the limited formalism of so many recent works, and that it

reclaim a cultural base and the most complete possible reading of the past.
(Cited by Portoghesi 1982, 89)

That reading of the past can be done in many moods and with varying degrees of complexity. The range is clear in the work of Robert Venturi. Its parodic and ironic recycling of historical forms aims not just at double encoding but at dual communication, both to the minority of architects and historians who will see all this parodic play and to the public at large. It intends to provoke reaction in *all* viewers.

In this context, it is not accidental that Jencks (1980a, 181) should decide to mention T. S. Eliot in conjunction with the Post-Modernist desire to change our way of seeing the past. As in Eliot's verse, there is a high degree of engagement of the decoder, combined with a high degree of textual complexity. And parody is central to both. If Post-Modernist theorists do not often use the word parody itself, I would argue that this is because of the strong negative interdiction that parody is still under because of its trivialization through the inclusion of ridicule in its definition. These architects clearly do not want to make fun of the past. Their "vision of interconnectedness" (Russell 1980, 189) is what makes them part not only of a recent postmodernist consciousness, but of the aesthetic consciousness of our entire century.

Parody today is endowed with the power to renew. It need not do so, but it can. We must never forget the hybrid nature of parody's connection with the "world," the mixture of conservative and revolutionary impulses in both aesthetic and social terms. What has traditionally been called parody privileges the normative impulse, but today's art abounds as well in examples of parody's power to revitalize. In Leo Steinberg's words:

> There are instances by the score where the artist invests the work he takes from with renewed relevance; he bestows on it a viability hitherto unsuspected; he actualizes its potentialities like a Brahms borrowing themes from Handel or Haydn. He can clear cobwebs away and impart freshness to things that were moldering in neglect or, what is worse, had grown banal through false familiarity. By altering their environment, a latter-day artist can lend moribund images a new lease on life. (1978, 25)

That this renewal can have social implications is as clear in Post-Modernist architecture as it is in novels such as *The French Lieutenant's Woman* or *Famous Last Words*. Since I believe that there are no completely transhistorical definitions of parody possible, it follows that the social or "worldly" status of parody can also never be fixed or finally and permanently defined. But the "world" does not disappear in the "inter-art traffic" that is parody. Through interaction with satire, through the pragmatic need for encoder and decoder to share codes, and through the paradox of its authorized transgression, the parodic appropriation of the past reaches out beyond textual introversion and aesthetic narcissism to address the "text's situation in the world."

If this is true, then surely parody must be taken more seriously than some critics still permit. Jonathan Culler, for instance, describes the "spirit" of parody as: "I see how this poem works; look how easy it is to show up the sententiousness of this poem; its effects are imitable and hence artificial; its achievement is fragile and depends on conventions of reading being taken seriously" (1975, 153). What is needed here is a broader notion of the conventions of reading, and such an expanded notion must be based to some extent on the kinds of texts read. In other words, it is in actually looking to the didactic parodic texts of modern art that we can come to discover the true "spirit" of parody. This is why my so-called "theory" of parody is derived from the teachings of the texts themselves, rather than from any theoretical structure imposed from without. Parody today cannot be explained *totally* in structuralist terms of form, in the hermeneutic context of response, in a semiotic-ideological framework, or in a post-structuralist absorption of everything into textuality. Yet the complex determinants of parody in some way involve all of these current critical perspectives – and many more. It is in this way that parody can, inadvertently perhaps, serve another useful function today: it can call into question the temptation toward the monolithic in modern theory. If many perspectives help us understand this pervasive modern phenomenon, but if none is sufficient in itself, then how could we claim that a structuralist, semiotic, hermeneutic, or deconstructive approach was in itself totally adequate to the task? This is not so much an argument for critical pluralism as it is a plea for theory that is a response to aesthetic realities.

Our parodies are ended. These our authors,
As we foretold you, were all Spirits, and
Are melted into air, into thin air.
And, like the baseless fabric of these verses,
The Critic's puff, The Trade's advertisement,
The Patron's promise, and the World's applause, –
Yea, all the hopes of poets, – shall dissolve,
And, like this unsubstantial fable fated,
Leave not a groat behind!

Horace Twiss

BIBLIOGRAPHY

Abastado, Claude (1976) "Situation de la parodie," *Cahiers du XXe Siècle*, 6, 9-37.

Albalat, Antoine (1910) *La Formation du style par l'assimilation des auteurs.* Paris: A. Colin.

Albertsen, L. L. (1971) "Der Begriff Pastiche," *Orbis Litterarum*, 26, 1-8.

Alleman, Beda (1956) *Ironie und Dichtung.* Pfullingen: Neske.

———— (1978) "De l'ironie en tant que principe littéraire," *Poétique*, 36, 385-98.

Almansi, Guido (1978) "L'Affaire mystérieuse de l'abominable 'tongue-in-cheek,' " *Poétique*, 36, 413-26.

Alter, Robert (1975) *Partial Magic: The Novel as a Self-Conscious Genre.* Berkeley, Ca: University of California Press.

Altmann, Peter (1977) *Sinfonia von Luciano Berio: eine analytische Studie.* Vienna: Universal.

Amis, Kingsley (1978) "Introduction" to *New Oxford Book of Light Verse.* London: Oxford University Press.

Amossy, Ruth, and Rosen, Elisheva (1974) "La Dame aux catleyas: fonction du pastiche et de la parodie dans *A la recherche du temps perdu,"* *Littérature*, 14, 55-76.

Antin, David (1980) "Is there a Postmodernism?" in Garvin (1980), 127-35.

Apple, Max (1976) *The Oranging of America and Other Stories.* New York: Grossman.

Aquin, Hubert (1972) *Prochain Episode*, trans. Penny Williams. Toronto: McClelland & Stewart.

Atwood, Margaret (1976) *Lady Oracle.* Toronto: McClelland & Stewart.

Auden, W. H. (1968) *The Dyer's Hand.* New York: Vintage.

Auerbach, Erich (1957) *Mimesis*, trans. Willard Trask. Garden City, NY: Doubleday.

Austen, Jane (1910) *Northanger Abbey.* London: Chatto & Windus.

———— (1922) *Love and Friendship.* London: Chatto & Windus.

Bakhtin, Mikhail (1968) *Rabelais and his World*, trans. Hélène Iswolsky. Cambridge, Mass.: MIT Press.

——— (1973) *Problems of Dostoevsky's Poetics*, trans. R. W. Rotsel. Ann Arbor, Mich.: Ardis.

——— (1978) *Esthétique et théorie du roman*, trans. Daria Olivier. Paris: Gallimard.

——— (1981) *The Dialogic Imagination*, trans. Caryl Emerson, Michael Holquist, ed. Michael Holquist. Austin, Tex., and London: University of Texas Press.

[Bakhtin, Mikhail]/Vološinov, V. N. (1973) *Marxism and the Philosophy of Language*, trans. Ladislav Matejka and I. R. Titunik. New York and London: Seminar Press.

Banville, John (1971) *Nightspawn*. London: Secker & Warburg.

——— (1973) *Birchwood*. London: Secker & Warburg.

Barber, Bruce Alistair (1983-4) "Appropriation/Expropriation: Convention or Intervention," *Parachute*, 33, 29-39.

——— (ed.) (1983) *Essays on [Performance] and Cultural Politicization*, *Open Letter*, 5th series, Nos 5-6.

Barth, John (1960) *The Sot-Weed Factor*. New York: Doubleday.

——— (1967) "The Literature of Exhaustion," *Atlantic* (August), 98-133.

——— (1968) *Lost in the Funhouse*. New York: Doubleday.

——— (1980) "The Literature of Replenishment: Postmodernist Fiction," *Atlantic* (January), 65-71.

——— (1982) "Some Reasons Why I Tell the Stories I Tell the Way I Tell Them Rather Than Some Other Sort of Stories Some Other Way," *New York Times Book Review* (9 May), 3, 29-31, 33.

Barthes, Roland (1972a) "The Death of the Author," in S. Sears and G. W. Lord (eds), *The Discontinuous Universe*. New York: Basic Books.

——— (1972b) *Critical Essays*, trans. Richard Howard. Evanston, Ill.: Northwestern University Press.

——— (1974) *S/Z*, trans. Richard Miller. New York: Hill & Wang.

——— (1975a) *Roland Barthes*. Paris: Seuil.

——— (1975b) *The Pleasure of the Text*, trans. Richard Miller. New York: Hill & Wang.

Bate, W. Jackson (1970) *The Burden of the Past and the English Poet*. Cambridge, Mass.: Belknap Press/Harvard University Press.

Bauerle, Ruth (1967) "A Sober Drunken Speech: Stephen's Parodies in 'The Oxen of the Sun,'" *James Joyce Quarterly*, 5, 40-6.

Beerbohm, Max (1921) *A Christmas Garland*. London: Heinemann.

——— (1970) *Last Theatres, 1904-1910*. London: Rupert Hart-Davis.

Belsey, Catherine (1980) *Critical Practice*. London and New York: Methuen.

Benamou, Michel (1977) "Presence and Play," in Benamou and Carmello (1977), 3-7.

Benamou, Michel, and Carmello, Charles (eds) (1977) *Performance in Postmodern*

Culture. Milwaukee, Wisc.: Center for Twentieth Century Studies.

Ben-Porat, Ziva (1976) "The Poetics of Literary Allusion," *PTL*, 1, 105-28.

────── (1979) "Method in *Madness*: Notes on the Structure of Parody, Based on MAD TV Satires," *Poetics Today*, 1, 245-72.

Benstock, Shari (1983) "At the Margin of Discourse: Footnotes in the Fictional Text," *PMLA*, 98, 204-25.

Berlin, Normand (1973) "*Rosencrantz and Guildenstern are Dead:* Theater of Criticism," *Modern Drama*, 16, 269-77.

Bernadac, Marie-Laure (1983) "De Manet à Picasso: l'éternel retour," in *Bonjour Monsieur Manet*, 33-46. Paris: Centre Georges Pompidou.

Berto, Giuseppe (1964) *Il male oscuro*. Milan: Rizzoli.

Bethea, David H., and Davydov, Sergei (1981) "Pushkin's Saturnine Cupid: The Poetics of Parody in *The Tales of Belkin*," *PMLA*, 96, 8-21.

Bilous, Daniel (1982) "Récrire l'intertexte: La Bruyère pasticheur de Montaigne," *Cahiers de littérature du XVIIe siècle*, 4, 106-14.

────── (1983) "Intertexte/Pastiche: L'Intermimotexte," *Texte*, 2, 135-60.

Blackmur, Richard P. (1964) "Parody and Critique: Mann's *Doctor Faustus*," in *Eleven Essays in the European Novel*, 97-116. New York: Harcourt, Brace & World.

Bloom, Edward A., and Bloom, Lillian D. (1979) *Satire's Persuasive Voice*. Ithaca, NY: Cornell University Press.

Bloom, Harold (1973) *The Anxiety of Influence: A Theory of Poetry*. New York: Oxford University Press.

Bond, Richmond Pugh (1932) *English Burlesque Poetry, 1700-1750*. Cambridge, Mass.: Harvard University Press.

Bonfel'd, Marina (1977) "Parodija v muzyke venskih klassikov," *Sovetskaja Muzyka*, 5, 99-102.

Booth, Wayne C. (1961) *The Rhetoric of Fiction*. Chicago, Ill.: University of Chicago Press.

────── (1974) *A Rhetoric of Irony*. Chicago, Ill.: University of Chicago Press.

────── (1982) "Freedom and Interpretation: Bakhtin and the Challenge of Feminist Criticism," *Critical Inquiry*, 9, 45-76.

Borges, Jorge Luis (1962, 1964) *Labyrinths*, ed. Donald A. Yates and James E. Irby. New York: New Directions.

────── (1970) *The Aleph and Other Stories 1933-1969*, trans. Norman Thomas di Giovanni. New York: Dutton.

Boston, Richard (1969) "John Fowles, Alone But Not Lonely," *New York Times Book Review* (9 November), 2, 52, 54.

Bouché, Claude (1976) "Lautréamont: l'enjeu d'une écriture parodique," *Cahiers du XXe siècle*, 6, 39-51.

Boyle, Robert, SJ (1970) "Swiftian Allegory and Dantean Parody in Joyce's 'Grace,' " *James Joyce Quarterly*, 7, 11-21.

Brecht, Bertolt (1974) "Against George Lukács," *New Left Review*, 84, 39-53.

────── (1979) *Collected Plays*, 2, ii, and 2, iii, ed. John Willet and Ralph

Manheim. London: Eyre Methuen.

Brower, Robert H., and Miner, Earl (1961) *Japanese Court Poetry*. Stanford, Ca: Stanford University Press.

Buchloh, Benjamin H. D. (1982) "Parody and Appropriation in Francis Picabia, Pop, and Sigmar Polke," *Artforum*, 20 (7), 28-34.

—— (1983) "Allegorical Procedures: Appropriation and Montage in Contemporary Art," in Barber (1983), 164-93.

Burden, Robert (1979) "The Novel Interrogates Itself: Parody as Self-Consciousness in Contemporary English Fiction," in Malcolm Bradbury and David Palmer (eds), *The Contemporary English Novel*. Stratford-upon-Avon Studies 18, 133-55. London: Edward Arnold.

Burke, Kenneth (1967) *The Philosophy of Literary Form: Studies in Symbolic Action*. 2nd edn. Baton Rouge, La: Louisiana State University Press.

Butler, Christopher (1980) *After the Wake: An Essay on the Contemporary Avant-Garde*. Oxford: Clarendon Press.

Butor, Michel (1967) "La Critique et l'invention," *Critique*, 247, 283-95.

Cabrera Infante, Guillermo (1971) *Three Trapped Tigers*, trans. Donald Gardner and Suzanne Jill Levine. New York: Harper & Row.

Calinescu, Matei (1980) "Ways of Looking at Fiction," in Garvin (1980), 155-70.

Calvino, Italo (1981) *If on a Winter's Night a Traveler*, trans. William Weaver. Toronto: Lester & Orpen Dennys.

Carlisle, Henry C., Jr (ed.) (1962) *American Satire in Prose and Verse*. New York: Random House.

Caute, David (1972) *The Illusion*. New York: Harper & Row.

Chambers, Robert William, Jr (1974) "Parodic Perspectives: A Theory of Parody," PhD Dissertation, Indiana University.

Chatman, Seymour (1979) *Story and Discourse*. Ithaca, NY: Cornell University Press.

Clair, Jean (1974) "Erostrate ou le musée en question," *L'Art de masse n'existe pas, Revue d'esthétique*, 3-4, 185-206.

Clark, John R., and Motto, Anna Lydia (eds) (1973) *Satire: That Blasted Art*. New York: Putnam's.

Clay, Jean (1983) "Onguents, fards, pollens," in *Bonjour Monsieur Manet*, 6-24. Paris: Centre Georges Pompidou.

Cobley, Evelyn (1984) "Sameness and Difference in Literary Repetition," *Recherches sémiotiques/Semiotic Inquiry*, 4.

Cohen, Leonard (1970) *Beautiful Losers*. Toronto: McClelland & Stewart.

Compagnon, Antoine (1979) *La Seconde Main ou le travail de la citation*. Paris: Seuil.

Cone, Edward T. (1960) "Analysis Today," *Musical Quarterly*, 46, 172-88.

Conrad, Peter (1980) "Chewing up the Soft Machine," *The Times Literary Supplement* (30 May), 613.

Conte, Gian Biagio (1974) *Memoria dei poeti e sistema letterario*. Turin: Einaudi.

Contini, Gianfranco (1970) *Varianti e altra linguistica*. Turin: Einaudi.

122   *A Theory of Parody*

Courtney, E. (1962) "Parody and Literary Allusion in Menippean Satire," *Philologus*, 106, 86-100.

Culler, Jonathan (1975) *Structuralist Poetics: Structuralism, Linguistics and the Study of Literature*. London: Routledge & Kegan Paul.

———— (1981) *The Pursuit of Signs*. Ithaca, NY: Cornell University Press.

———— (1982) *On Deconstruction: Theory and Criticism after Structuralism*. Ithaca, NY: Cornell University Press.

Dali, Salvador (1963) *Le Mythe tragique de l'Angélus de Millet: interprétation "paranoïaque-critique."* Paris: Pauvert.

Dällenbach, Lucien (1976) "Intertexte et autotexte," *Poétique*, 27, 282-96.

Dane, Joseph A. (1980) "Parody and Satire: A Theoretical Model," *Genre*, 13, 145-59.

Davidson, Israel (1966) *Parody in Jewish Literature*. New York: AMS Press.

Davis, Joe Lee (1951) "Criticism and Parody," *Thought*, 26, 180-204.

Deffoux, Léon L. (1932) *Le Pastiche littéraire des origines à nos jours*. Paris: Librairie Delagrave.

Deleuze, Gilles (1968) *Différence et répétition*. Paris: Presses Universitaires de France.

Derrida, Jacques (1968) "La Différence," in *Tel Quel: Théorie d'ensemble*, 41-66. Paris: Seuil.

———— (1978) *Writing and Difference*. Chicago, Ill.: University of Chicago Press.

D'Israeli, Isaac (1886) "A Chapter on Parodies," in Hamilton (1884-9), 1-2.

Dooley, David J. (1971) *Contemporary Satire*. Toronto: Holt, Rinehart & Winston.

Dryden, John (1962) *Of Dramatic Poesy and Other Critical Essays*, 2 vols, ed. George Watson. London: Dent.

Dupréel, E. (1928) "Le Problème sociologique du rire," *Revue philosophique*, 106, 213-60.

Dupriez, Bernard (1977) *Gradus: Les Procédés littéraires*. Paris: UGE, 10/18.

Eagleton, Terry (1983) *Literary Theory: An Introduction*. Oxford: Basil Blackwell.

Easson, Angus (1970) "Parody as Comment in James Joyce's 'Clay,' " *James Joyce Quarterly*, 7, 75-81.

Eastman, Max (1936) *Enjoyment of Laughter*. New York: Simon & Schuster.

Eco, Umberto (1979) *The Role of the Reader*. Bloomington, Ind.: Indiana University Press.

———— (1983) *The Name of the Rose*, trans. William Weaver. New York: Harcourt, Brace, Jovanovich.

Eichner, Hans (1952) "Aspects of Parody in the Works of Thomas Mann," *Modern Language Review*, 47, 30-48.

Eidson, John Olin (1970) "Parody," in Joseph T. Shipley (ed.), *Dictionary of World Literary Terms*, 231-2. London: Allen & Unwin.

Èjxenbaum, Boris M. (1965) "La Théorie de la 'méthode formelle,' " in Todorov (1965), 31-75.

———— (1978a) "Literary Environment," in Matejka and Pomorska (1978), 56-65.

—— (1978b) "O. Henry and the Theory of the Short Story," in Matejka and Pomorska (1978), 227-70.

Eliot, T. S. (1940) *The Waste Land and Other Poems*. London: Faber & Faber.

—— (1966) "Tradition and the Individual Talent," in *Selected Essays*, 13-22. London: Faber & Faber.

Empson, William (1963) *Seven Types of Ambiguity*, 3rd edn. London: Chatto & Windus.

Erlich, Victor (1955, 1965) *Russian Formalism: History–Doctrine*. New Haven, Conn.: Yale University Press.

Falk, Robert Paul (1955) *American Literature in Parody*. New York: Twayne.

Farrer, J. A. (1907) *Literary Forgeries*. London: Longmans, Green.

Faulkner, William (1930) *As I Lay Dying*. New York: Random House.

Federman, Raymond (1977) "Federman: Voices within Voices," in Benamou and Carmello (1977), 159-98.

—— (ed.) (1981) *Surfiction: Fiction Now...and Tomorrow*, 2nd edn. Chicago, Ill.: Swallow Press.

Feinberg, Leonard (1963) *The Satirist: His Temperament, Motivation, and Influence*. Ames, Iowa: Iowa State University Press.

—— (1967) *Introduction to Satire*. Ames, Iowa: Iowa State University Press.

Felstiner, John (1972) *The Lies of Art: Max Beerbohm's Parody and Caricature*. New York: Knopf.

Fiedler, Leslie A. (1965) *Waiting for the End: The American Literary Scene from Hemingway to Baldwin*. London: Cape.

Finscher, Ludwig, and Dadelsen, Georg von (1962) "Parodie und Kontrafactur," in F. Blume (ed.), *Die Musik in Geschichte und Gegenwart: Allgemeine Enzyklopädie der Musik*, X, 815-34. Basle: Bärenreiter Kassel.

Fish, Stanley (1980) *Is There a Text in this Class?* Cambridge, Mass.: Harvard University Press.

—— (1982) "Working on the Chain Gang: Interpretation in the Law and Literary Criticism," *Critical Inquiry*, 9, 201-16.

Flaubert, Gustave (1964) *Bouvard et Pécuchet*. Paris: Nizet.

Forrest-Thomson, Veronica (1978) *Poetic Artifice: A Theory of Twentieth-Century Poetry*. New York: St Martin's Press.

Foster, Richard (1956) "Wilde as Parodist: A Second Look at *The Importance of Being Earnest*," *College English*, 18, 18-23.

Foucault, Michel (1970) *The Order of Things*. New York: Random House.

—— (1972) *The Archaeology of Knowledge*, trans. Alan Sheridan. London: Tavistock; New York: Pantheon.

—— (1977) *Language, Counter-Memory, Practice*, trans. Donald F. Bouchard and Sherry Smith. Ithaca, NY: Cornell University Press.

—— (1983) *This is not a Pipe*, trans. James Harkness. Berkeley, Ca: University of California Press.

Fourcade, Dominique (1983) "Matisse et Manet?" in *Bonjour Monsieur Manet*, 25-32. Paris: Centre Georges Pompidou.

Fowles, John (1964) *The Aristos*. Boston, Mass.: Little, Brown.
—— (1968) "Notes on Writing a Novel," *Harper's Magazine* (July), 88-97.
—— (1969a) *The French Lieutenant's Woman*. Boston, Mass.: Little, Brown.
—— (1969b) "On Writing a Novel," *Cornhill Magazine*, 1060, 281-90.
—— (1969c) "Notes on an Unfinished Novel," in Thomas McCormack (ed.), *Afterwords: Novelists on their Novels*, 160-75. New York: Harper & Row.
—— (1974) *The Ebony Tower*. Boston, Mass.: Little, Brown.
Freeman, Rosemary (1963) "Parody as a Literary Form: George Herbert and Wilfred Owen," *Essays in Criticism*, 13, 307-22.
Freidenberg, O. M. (1974, 1975) "The Origin of Parody," in Henryk Baran (ed.), *Semiotics and Structuralism: Readings from the Soviet Union*. White Plains, NY: International Arts and Sciences Press.
Freud, Sigmund (1953-74) *The Standard Edition of the Complete Psychological Works of Sigmund Freud*, 24 vols. London: Hogarth Press and the Institute of Psycho-Analysis.
Freund, Winfried (1977) "Zur Theorie und Rezeption der Parodie: am Beispiel moderner lyrischer Parodien," *Sprache im technischen Zeitalter*, 62, 182-94.
—— (1981) *Die literarische Parodie*. Stuttgart: Metzler.
Frye, Dean (1965) "The Question of Shakespearean 'Parody,' " *Essays in Criticism*, 15, 22-6.
Frye, Northrop (1963) *The Educated Imagination*. Toronto: CBC Publications.
—— (1970) *The Anatomy of Criticism*. New York: Atheneum.
Gardner, John (1971) *Grendel*. New York: Ballantine.
Garvin, Harry R. (ed.) (1980) *Romanticism, Modernism, Postmodernism*. Lewisburg, Pa: Bucknell University Press.
Genette, Gérard (1979) *Introduction à l'architexte*. Paris: Seuil.
—— (1982) *Palimpsestes*. Paris: Seuil.
Gide, André (1973) *The Counterfeiters*, trans. Dorothy Bussy. New York: Vintage.
Gilbert, Sandra M. (1983) "In Yeats's House: The Death and Resurrection of Sylvia Plath," paper presented to McMaster English Seminar, Facets of Feminist Criticism (28 October).
Gilbert, Sandra M., and Gubar, Susan (1979) *The Madwoman in the Attic: The Woman Writer and the Nineteenth-Century Literary Imagination*. New Haven, Conn.: Yale University Press.
Gilbert, Stuart (1930) *James Joyce's Ulysses*. New York: Knopf.
Gilman, Sander L. (1974) *The Parodic Sermon in European Perspective*. Wiesbaden: Franz Steiner.
—— (1976) *Nietzschean Parody*. Bonn: Bouvier Verlag/Herbert Grundmann.
Goethe, Johann Wolfgang von (1948) *Gedenkausgabe*, XXI, ed. Ernst Beutler. Zürich: Artemis.
Golopenţia-Eretescu, Sanda (1969) "Grammaire de la parodie," *Cahiers de linguistique théorique et appliquée*, 6, 167-81.
Gomez-Moriana, Antonio (1980-1) "Intertextualité, interdiscursivité et parodie:

pour une sémanalyse du roman picaresque," *Canadian Journal of Research in Semiotics*, 8, 15-32.

Grannis, V. B. (1931) *Dramatic Parody in Eighteenth-Century France*. New York: Publications of the Institute of French Studies.

Gray, Alasdair (1981) *Lanark*. New York: Harper & Row.

Greene, Thomas M. (1982) *The Light in Troy: Imitation and Discovery in Renaissance Poetry*. New Haven, Conn.: Yale University Press.

Greig, J. Y. T. (1969) *The Psychology of Laughter and Comedy*. New York: Cooper Square.

Grice, H. P. (1975) "Logic and Conversation," in *Syntax and Semantics 3: Speech Acts*, 41-58. New York: Academic.

Groupe MU (1970) *Rhétorique générale*. Paris: Larousse.

—— (1978) "Ironique et iconique," *Poétique*, 36, 427-42.

—— (1979) "Iconique et plastique, sur un fondement de la rhétorique visuelle," *Rhétoriques, sémiotiques, Revue d'esthétique*, 1-2, 173-92.

Grout, Donald Jay (1980) *A History of Western Music*, 3rd edn. New York: Norton.

Gruber, Gerndt (1977) "Das musikalische Zitat als historisches und systematisches Problem," *Musicologica Austriaca*, 1, 121-35.

Hamilton, Walter (1884-9) *Parodies of the Works of English and American Authors*, 5 vols. London: Reeves & Turner.

Harder, Kelsie B. (1956) "Chaucer's Use of the Mystery Plays in the *Miller's Tale*," *Modern Language Quarterly*, 17, 193-8.

Hathaway, Baxter (1968) *Marvels and Commonplaces: Renaissance Literary Criticism*. New York: Random House.

Havens, R. D. (1961) *The Influence of Milton on English Poetry*. New York: Russell & Russell.

Hawthorne, Nathaniel (1960) *The Scarlet Letter*. Boston, Mass.: Houghton Mifflin.

Heller, Erich (1958a) *The Ironic German: A Study of Thomas Mann*. London: Secker & Warburg.

—— (1958b) "Parody, Tragic and Comic: Mann's *Doctor Faustus* and *Felix Krull*," *Sewanee Review*, 66, 519-46.

Hemingway, Ernest (1954) *The Sun also Rises*. New York: Scribner.

Hempel, Wido (1965) "Parodie, Travestie und Pastiche. Zur Geschichte von Wort und Sache," *Germanisch-Romanisch Monatsschrift*, 46, 150-76.

Hess, Thomas B. (1974) "The Art Comics of Ad Reinhardt," *Artforum*, 12 (8), 46-51.

Highet, Gilbert (1962) *The Anatomy of Satire*. Princeton, NJ: Princeton University Press.

Hirsch, E. D., Jr (1967) *Validity in Interpretation*. New Haven, Conn.: Yale University Press.

Hobbes, Thomas (1839) *The English Works of Thomas Hobbes*, IV, ed. William Molesworth. London: John Bohn.

Hoffmann, Gerhard, Hornung, Alfred, and Kunow, Rüdiger (1977) " 'Modern,' 'Postmodern' and 'Contemporary' as Criteria for the Analysis of Twentieth-Century Literature," *Amerikastudien*, 22, 19-46.

Hofstadter, Douglas (1979) *Gödel, Escher, Bach: An Eternal Golden Braid.* New York: Basic.

Honsa, William M., Jr (1974) "Parody and Narrator in Thomas Mann's *Dr Faustus* and *The Holy Sinner*," *Orbis Litterarum*, 29, 61-76.

Householder, Fred W., Jr (1944) "Parodia," *Classical Philology*, 39, 1-9.

Hughes, Robert (1980) *The Shock of the New: Art and the Century of Change.* London: BBC.

Hutcheon, Linda (1980) *Narcissistic Narrative: The Metafictional Paradox.* Waterloo, Ont.: Wilfrid Laurier University Press. Pbk edn 1984, New York and London: Methuen.

—— (1983) "The Carnivalesque and Contemporary Narrative: Popular Culture and the Erotic," *University of Ottawa Quarterly*, 53 (1), 83-94.

Hutcheon, Linda, and Butler, Sharon (1981) "The Literary Semiotics of Verbal Irony: The Example of Joyce's 'The Boarding House,' " *Recherches sémiotiques/ Semiotic Inquiry*, 1, 244-60.

Idt, Geneviève (1972-3) "La Parodie: rhétorique ou lecture?" in *Le Discours et le sujet*, 128-73. Nanterre: Université de Paris X.

Imhof, Rüdiger (1981) " 'My Readers, that Small Band, Deserve a Rest': An Interview with John Banville," *Irish University Review*, 11, 5-12.

Iser, Wolfgang (1978) *The Act of Reading: A Theory of Aesthetic Response.* Baltimore, Md: Johns Hopkins University Press.

Jacobs, Jane (1961) *The Death and Life of Great American Cities.* New York: Vintage.

Jakobson, Roman (1960) "Closing Statement: Linguistics and Poetics," in Thomas A. Sebeok (ed.), *Style in Language*, 350-77. Cambridge, Mass.: MIT Press.

Jameson, Fredric (1981) *The Political Unconscious.* Ithaca, NY: Cornell University Press.

Jarrell, Mackie L. (1957) "Joyce's Use of Swift's *Polite Conversation* in the 'Circe' Episode of *Ulysses*," *PMLA*, 72, 545-54.

Jauss, Hans Robert (1967) *Literaturgeschichte als Provokation der Literaturwissenschaft.* Constance: Universitätsverlag.

Jencks, Charles (1977) *The Language of Post-Modern Architecture.* London: Academy.

—— (1980a) *Late-Modern Architecture and Other Essays.* London: Academy.
—— (1980b) *Post-Modern Classicism: The New Synthesis.* London: Academy.

Jencks, Charles, and Chaitkin, William (1982) *Architecture Today.* New York: Abrams.

Jenny, Laurent (1976) "La Stratégie de la forme," *Poétique*, 27, 257-81.

Jerrold, Walter, and Leonard, R. M. (eds) (1913) *A Century of Parody and Imitation.* London: Oxford University Press.

Johnson, Samuel (1806) *A Dictionary of the English Language*, II, 9th edn. London: J. Johnson, etc.

Josephson, N. S. (1975) "Kanon und Parodie: zu einigen Josquin-Nachahmungen," *Tijdschrift der vereeniging voor nederlandsche muziekgeschiedenis*, 25 (2), 23-32.

Josipovici, Gabriel (1964) "*Lolita*: Parody and the Pursuit of Beauty," *Critical Quarterly*, 6, 35-48.

Joyce, James (1959) *Finnegans Wake*. New York: Viking.

——— (1961) *Dubliners*. New York: Viking.

——— (1964) *A Portrait of the Artist as a Young Man*. New York: Viking.

——— (1966) *Ulysses*. New York: Vintage.

Jump, John D. (1972) *Burlesque*. London and New York: Methuen.

Kant, Immanuel (1957) *Werke*, V, ed. Wilhelm Weischedel. Frankfurt: Insel.

Karrer, Wolfgang (1977) *Parodie, Travestie, Pastiche*. Munich: Wilhelm Fink.

Kawin, Bruce R. (1972) *Telling It Again and Again: Repetition in Literature and Film*. Ithaca, NY: Cornell University Press.

Kennedy, J. Gerald (1980) "Parody as Exorcism: 'The Raven' and 'The Jewbird,' " *Genre*, 13, 161-9.

Kenner, Hugh (1964) *Flaubert, Joyce and Beckett: The Stoic Comedians*. London: W. H. Allen.

Kerbrat-Orecchioni, Catherine (1976) "Problèmes de l'ironie," *Linguistique et sémiologie*, 2, 16-27.

——— (1977) *La Connotation*. Lyon: Presses Universitaires Lyon.

——— (1980) "L'Ironie comme trope," *Poétique*, 41, 108-27.

Kerenyi, K. (1956) "Die goldene Parodie: Randbemerkungen zu den 'Vertauschten Köpfen,' " *Die neue Rundschau*, 67, 549-56.

Kiremidjian, G. D. (1969) "The Aesthetics of Parody," *Journal of Aesthetics and Art Criticism*, 28, 231-42.

Kitchin, George (1931) *A Survey of Burlesque and Parody in English*. Edinburgh and London: Oliver & Boyd.

Klein, Robert (1970) *La Forme et l'intelligible*. Paris: Gallimard.

Kneif, Tibor (1973) "Zur Semantik des musikalischen Zitats," *Neue Zeitschrift für Musik*, 134, 3-9.

Koller, H. (1956) "Die Parodie," *Glotta*, 35, 17-32.

Kris, Ernst (1964) *Psychoanalytic Explorations in Art*. New York: Schocken.

Kristeva, Julia (1968) "Problèmes de la structuration du texte," in *Tel Quel: Théorie d'ensemble*, 297-316. Paris: Seuil.

——— (1969) Σημειωτικὴ: *Recherches pour une sémanalyse*. Paris: Seuil.

——— (1974) *La Révolution du langage poétique*. Paris: Seuil.

——— (1980a) *Desire in Language*, trans. Thomas Gora, Alice Jardine, Leon S. Roudiez. New York: Columbia University Press.

——— (1980b) "Postmodernism?" in Garvin (1980), 136-41.

Kroetsch, Robert (1970) *The Studhorse Man*. New York: Simon & Schuster.

Kuhn, Clemens (1972) *Das Zitat in der Musik der Gegenwart*. Hamburg: Wagner.

Kuhn, Hans (1974) "Was parodiert die Parodie?" *Die neue Rundschau*, 85, 600-18.

Lawler, Traugott (1974) " 'Wafting Vapours from the Land of Dreams': Virgil's Fourth and Sixth Eclogues and the *Dunciad*," *Studies in English Literature 1500-1900*, 14, 373-86.

Leacock, Stephen (1937) *Humour and Humanity*. London: Thornton Butterworth.

Lee, Guy (1971) *Allusion, Parody and Imitation*. Hull: University of Hull.

Lehmann, Paul (1963) *Die Parodie im Mittelalter*. Stuttgart: Hiersemann.

Lelièvre, F. J. (1954) "The Basis of Ancient Parody," *Greece and Rome*, 1, 66-81.

——— (1958) "Parody in Juvenal and T. S. Eliot," *Classical Philology*, 53, 22-6.

Lem, Stanislaw (1978, 1979) *A Perfect Vacuum*, trans. Michael Kandel. New York and London: Harcourt, Brace & Jovanovich.

Lentricchia, Frank (1980) *After the New Criticism*. Chicago, Ill.: University of Chicago Press. Pbk edn 1983, London: Methuen.

Levin, Harry (1941) *James Joyce: A Critical Introduction*. Norfolk, Conn.: New Directions.

Levine, Jacob (1969) *Motivation in Humor*. New York: Atherton Press.

Lipman, Jean, and Marshall, Richard (1978) *Art about Art*. New York: Dutton.

Litz, A. Walton (1965) *Jane Austen: A Study of her Artistic Development*. New York: Oxford University Press.

Lodge, David (1965) *The British Museum is Falling Down*. London: McGibbon & Kee.

Lotman, Iouri (1973) *La Structure du texte artistique*, trans. Anne Fournier, Bernard Kreise, Eve Malleret, Joëlle Yong. Paris: Gallimard.

Lyotard, Jean-François (1979) *La Condition postmoderne: rapport sur le savoir*. Paris: Minuit.

Macdonald, Dwight (ed.) (1960) *Parodies: An Anthology from Chaucer to Beerbohm – and After*. New York: Random House.

McHale, Brian (1979) "Modernist Reading, Post-Modern Text: The Case of *Gravity's Rainbow*," *Poetics Today*, 1, 85-110.

Macherey, Pierre (1978) *A Theory of Literary Production*, trans. Geoffrey Wall. London: Routledge & Kegan Paul.

McLuhan, Marshall, and Watson, Wilfred (1970) "Parody," in *From Cliché to Archetype*, 167-70. New York. Viking.

Magritte, René (1979) *Écrits complets*, ed. André Blavier. Paris: Flammarion.

Malkoff, Karl (1967) "Allusion as Irony: Pound's Use of Dante in *Hugh Selwyn Mauberley*," *Minnesota Review*, 7, 81-8.

Manganelli, Giorgio (1967) *La letteratura come menzogna*. Milan: Feltrinelli.

Mann, Thomas (1948) *Doctor Faustus: The Life of the German Composer Adrian Leverkühn as Told by a Friend*, trans. H. T. Lowe-Porter. New York: Knopf.

——— (1955) *Confessions of Felix Krull, Confidence Man*, trans. Denver Lindley. New York: Knopf.

Markiewicz, Henryk (1967) "On the Definitions of Literary Parody," in *To Honour Roman Jakobson*, II, 1264-72. The Hague: Mouton.

Mars-Jones, Adam (1983) "Gilding the Unmentionables," *The Times Literary Supplement* (28 January), 179.

Martin, J. H. (1972) *Love's Fools: Aucassin, Troilus, Calisto and the Parody of the Courtly Lover*. London: Tamesis.

Martin, Loy D. (1980) "Literary Invention: The Illusion of Individual Talent," *Critical Inquiry*, 6, 649-67.

Matejka, Ladislav, and Pomorska, Krystyna (eds) (1978) *Readings in Russian Poetics*. Ann Arbor, Mich.: University of Michigan.

Meyer, Herman (1968) *The Poetics of Quotation in the European Novel*, trans. Theodore and Yetta Ziolkowski. Princeton, NJ: Princeton University Press.

Miller, Gerald R., and Bacon, Paula (1971) "Open- and Closed-Mindedness and Recognition of Visual Humor," *Journal of Communication*, 21, 150-9.

Moler, Kenneth L. (1968) *Jane Austen's Art of Allusion*. Lincoln, Neb.: University of Nebraska Press.

Molloy, Francis C. (1981) "The Search for Truth: The Fiction of John Banville," *Irish University Review*, 11, 29-51.

Monteilhet, Hubert (1975) *Mourir à Francfort*. Paris: Denoël.

Monter, Barbara Heldt (1968) "Koz'ma Prutkov and the Theory of Parody," PhD Dissertation, University of Chicago.

Morawski, Stefan (1970) "The Basic Functions of Quotation," in C. H. Van Schoonevelt (ed.), *Sign, Language, Culture*, 690-705. The Hague: Mouton.

Morgan, Owen, and Pagès, Alain (1980) "Une Pièce inconnue de Zola en 1879," *Zola: Thèmes et recherches (Cahiers de l'UGR Froissart)*, 5, 91-8.

Morgan, Robert P. (1977) "On the Analysis of Recent Music," *Critical Inquiry*, 4, 33-53.

Morier, Henri (1961) *Dictionnaire de poétique et de rhétorique*, 1st edn. Paris: Presses Universitaires de France.

Morris, Charles (1938) *Foundations of the Theory of Signs*, I. Chicago, Ill.: University of Chicago Press.

Morrison, Blake (1982) "The Pelvis on the Slab," *The Times Literary Supplement* (29 January), 111.

Morrissette, Bruce (1956) *The Great Rimbaud Forgery*. St Louis, Mo.: Washington University.

Morson, Gary Saul (1981) *The Boundaries of Genre: Dostoevsky's "Diary of a Writer" and the Traditions of Literary Utopia*. Austin, Tex.: University of Texas Press.

Morton, A. Q. (1978) *Literary Detection: How to Prove Authorship and Fraud in Literature and Documents*. London: Bowker.

Morton, Murray (1971) "A Paradise of Parodies," *Satire Newsletter*, 9, 33-42.

Moschini, Francesco (1979) "Notes on Paolo Portoghesi, Architect," in Francesco Moschini (ed.), *Paolo Portoghesi: Projects and Drawings 1949-79*, 7-13. New York: Rizzoli.

Muecke, D. C. (1969) *The Compass of Irony.* London: Methuen.
———— (1978) "Analyses de l'ironie," *Poétique,* 36, 478-94.
Murdoch, Iris (1961) *A Severed Head.* London: Chatto & Windus.
———— (1973) *The Black Prince.* London: Chatto & Windus.
Nabokov, Vladimir (1962) *Pale Fire.* New York: Putnam's.
———— (1969) *Ada or Ardor: A Family Chronicle.* New York: McGraw-Hill.
———— (1973) *Strong Opinions.* New York: McGraw-Hill.
Nehemas, Alexander (1981) "The Postulated Author: Critical Monism as a Regulative Ideal," *Critical Inquiry,* 8, 133-49.
Neumann, Robert (1927-8) "Zur Ästhetik der Parodie," *Die Literatur,* 30, 439-41.
Nichols, Bill (1981) *Ideology and the Image.* Bloomington, Ind.: Indiana University Press.
Nietzsche, Friedrich (1920-9) *Gesammelte Werke: Musarionausgabe,* IX. Munich: Musarion.
Nye, Robert (1980) *Faust.* London: Hamish Hamilton.
Oates, Joyce Carol (1982) *A Bloodsmoor Romance.* London: Cape.
Oliver, H. J. (1974) "Literary Allusions in Jacobean Drama," in J. A. Ward (ed.), *Renaissance Studies to Honor Carroll Camden,* 131-40. Houston, Tex.: Rice University.
Osolsobe, Ivo (1973) "K teorii parodie," *Slavica Slavaca,* 8, 374-85.
Painter, George D. (1965) *Proust: The Later Years.* Boston, Mass.: Little, Brown.
Patteson, Richard (1974) "What Stencil Knew: Structure and Certitude in Pynchon's *V.,*" *Critique,* 16, 30-44.
Paull, Harry Major (1928) *Literary Ethics.* London: Butterworth.
Paulson, Ronald (1967) *The Fictions of Satire.* Baltimore, Md: Johns Hopkins University Press.
Payant, René (1979) "Bricolage pictural: l'art à propos de l'art; I - La Question de la citation," *Parachute,* 16, 5-8.
———— (1980) "II - Citation et intertextualité," *Parachute,* 18, 25-32.
Perri, Carmela (1978) "On Alluding," *Poetics,* 7, 289-307.
Perri, Carmela, Carugati, G., Forndran, M., Mamaeva, A. G., Moody, E., Seligsohn, Z. Levine, Vinge, L., Wallace Costa, P., and Weinapple, F. (1979) "Allusion Studies: An International Annotated Bibliography, 1921-1977," *Style,* 13, 178-225.
Pfrimmer, Édouard (1971) "Brecht et la parodie: *Arturo Ui,*" *Études germaniques,* 26, 73-88.
Pöhlmann, Egert (1972) "Parodia," *Glotta,* 50, 144-56.
Poirier, Richard (1968) "The Politics of Self-Parody," *Partisan Review,* 35, 339-53.
Pontbriand, Chantal (ed.) (1981) *Performance: text(e)s & documents.* Montreal: Parachute.
Popovič, Anton (1976) "Aspects of Metatext," *Canadian Review of Comparative Literature,* 3, 225-35.

Portoghesi, Paolo (1974) *Le inibizioni dell'architettura*. Bari: Laterza.

—— (1979) "Architecture Born of Architecture," in Francesco Moschini (ed.), *Paolo Portoghesi: Projects and Drawings 1949-1979*, 15-16. New York: Rizzoli.

—— (1982) *After Modern Architecture*. New York: Rizzoli.

Postma, J. (1926) *Tennyson as Seen by his Parodists*. Amsterdam: H. J. Paris.

Pound, Ezra (1928) *Selected Poems*. London: Faber & Faber.

Preminger, Alex (ed.) (1974) *The Princeton Encyclopedia of Poetics*. Princeton, NJ: Princeton University Press.

Priestman, Judith (1980) "The Age of Parody: Literary Parody and Some Nineteenth Century Perspectives," PhD Dissertation, University of Kent at Canterbury.

Pütz, Manfred (1973) "The Struggle of the Postmodern," *Kritikon Litterarum*, 2, 225-37.

Quintilian (1922) *Institutio Oratoria*, trans. H. E. Butler. London: Heinemann; New York: Putnam's.

Rabinowitz, Peter J. (1980) " 'What's Hecuba to Us?': The Audience's Experience of Literary Borrowing," in Susan R. Suleiman and Inge Crosman (eds), *The Reader in the Text: Essays on Audience and Interpretation*, 241-63. Princeton, NJ: Princeton University Press.

—— (1981) "Fictional Music: Toward a Theory of Listening," in Harry R. Garvin (ed.), *Theories of Reading, Looking and Listening*, 193-208. Lewisburg, Pa: Bucknell University Press.

Rau, P. (1967) *Paratragödia*. Munich: C. H. Beck

Reiss, Timothy J. (1982) *The Discourse of Modernism*. Ithaca, NY: Cornell University Press.

Revzin, Isaac I. (1971) "Das Schema einer Sprache mit endlich vielen Zuständen und die Möglichkeiten, es in der Poetik anzuwenden (Zum Mechanismus der Parodie)," in Jens Ihwe (ed.), *Literaturwissenschaft und Linguistik*, II, 2, 587-602. Frankfurt am Main: Athenäum.

Ricardou, Jean (1972) "Naissance d'une fiction," in Jean Ricardou and Françoise van Rossum-Guyon (eds), *Nouveau Roman: hier, aujourd'hui*, I, 379-92. Paris: UGE, 10/18.

Richardson, Mrs Herbert (1935) *Parody*. English Association Pamphlet No. 92. Oxford: Oxford University Press.

Ricœur, Paul (1969) *Le Conflit des interprétations*. Paris: Seuil.

—— (1975) "Biblical Hermeneutics," *Semeia*, 4, 29-148.

Riewald, J. G. (1966) "Parody as Criticism," *Neophilologus*, 50, 125-48.

Riffaterre, Michael (1974) "The Poetic Functions of Intertextual Humor," *Romanic Review*, 65, 278-93.

—— (1978) *Semiotics of Poetry*. Bloomington, Ind.: Indiana University Press. Pbk edn 1980, London: Methuen.

—— (1979a) *La Production du texte*. Paris: Seuil.

—— (1979b) "Sémiotique intertextuelle: l'interprétant," *Rhétoriques, sémiotiques,*

Revue d'esthétique, 122-38. Paris: UGE, 10/18.

————— (1980a) "Syllepsis," *Critical Inquiry*, 6, 625-38.

————— (1980b) "La Trace de l'intertexte," *La Pensée*, 215, 4-18.

————— (1981a) "L'Intertexte inconnu," *Littérature*, 41, 4-7.

————— (1981b) "La Parodie à la lumière de la théorie de l'intertextualité," paper to Colloquium on the History and Theory of Parody, Queen's University (10 October).

Rimmon-Kenan, Shlomith (1980) "The Paradoxical Status of Repetition," *Poetics Today*, 1, 151-9.

Robbins, Tom (1976) *Even Cowgirls Get the Blues*. Boston, Mass.: Houghton Mifflin.

Röhrich, Lutz (1967) *Gebärde-Metapher-Parodie*. Düsseldorf: Schwann.

Rose, Margaret (1979) *Parody//Metafiction*. London: Croom Helm.

————— (1980) "Defining Parody," *Southern Review* (Adelaide), 13, 5-20.

Rosenthal, Harold, and Warrack, John (1964) *Dictionary of Music*. London: Oxford University Press.

Rosler, Martha (1983) "Notes on Quotes," in Barber (1983), 194-205.

Rotermund, Erwin (1963) *Die Parodie in der modernen deutschen Lyrik*. Munich: Eidos Verlag.

Rothenberg, Jerome (1977) "New Models, New Visions: Some Notes Toward a Poetics of Performance," in Benamou and Carmello (1977), 11-17.

Rovit, Earl (1963) "The Novel as Parody: John Barth," *Critique*, 6 (2), 77-85.

Rushdie, Salman (1981) *Midnight's Children*. London: Cape.

Russell, Charles (1980) "The Context of the Concept," in Garvin (1980), 181-93.

Said, Edward W. (1983) *The World, the Text, and the Critic*. Cambridge, Mass.: Harvard University Press.

Sarduy, Severo (1972) "Interview," *Diacritics*, 2 (2), 41-5.

Schiller, Friedrich von (1962) *Werke: Nationalausgabe*, XX: *Philosophische Schriften*, I, ed. Benno von Wiese. Weimar: Böhlau.

Schleusener, Jay (1980) "Convention and the Context of Reading," *Critical Inquiry*, 6, 669-80.

Schmid, Wolf, and Stempel, Wolf-Dieter (eds) (1983) *Dialog der Texte: Hamburger Kolloquium zur Intertextualität*. Vienna: Wiener Slawistischer Almanach.

Scholes, Robert (1969) "On Realism and Genre," *Novel*, 2, 269-73.

————— (1970) "Metafiction," *Iowa Review*, 1, 100-15.

Schonhorn, Manuel (1975) "*The Sun Also Rises*: I: The Jacob Allusion, II: Parody as Meaning," *Ball State University Forum*, 16 (2), 49-55.

Schopenhauer, Arthur (1949) *Sämtliche Werke*, II and III, ed. Arthur Hübscher. Wiesbaden: Brockhaus.

Searle, John (1969) *Speech Acts*. Cambridge: Cambridge University Press.

Shepperson, Archibald Bolling (1967) *The Novel in Motley: A History of the Burlesque Novel in English*. New York: Octagon.

Shlonsky, Tuvia (1966) "Literary Parody: Remarks on its Method and Function," in François Jost (ed.), *Proceedings of the IVth Congress of the International Comparative Literature Association*, II, 797-801. The Hague: Mouton.

Showalter, Elaine (1981) "Feminist Criticism in the Wilderness," *Critical Inquiry*, 8, 179-205.

Siegmund-Schultze, Walther (1977) "Das Zitat im zeitgenossischen Musikschaffen: eine produktivschopferische Traditionslinie?," *Musik und Gesellschaft*, 27 (2), 73-8.

Simon, Claude (1973) *Triptyque*. Paris: Minuit.

Šklovskij, Victor (1965) "Sterne's *Tristram Shandy*: Stylistic Commentary," in Lee T. Lemon and Marion J. Reis (eds), *Russian Formalist Criticism: Four Essays*, 25-57. Lincoln, Neb.: University of Nebraska Press.

——— (1973) "The Connection between Devices of *Syuzhet* Construction and General Stylistic Devices," in Stephen Bann and John E. Bowlt (eds), *Russian Formalism: 20th Century Studies*, 48-72. Edinburgh: Scottish Academic Press.

——— (1978) "The Mystery Novel: Dickens's *Little Dorrit*," in Matejka and Pomorska (1978), 220-6.

Smith, William Jay (1961) *The Spectra Hoax*. Middletown, Conn.: Wesleyan University Press.

Sonntag, Brunhilde (1977) *Untersuchungen zur Collage-Technik in der Musik des 20. Jahrhunderts*. Regensburg: Bosse.

Speirs, Ronald (1972) *Brecht's Early Plays*. London: Macmillan.

Sperber, Dan, and Wilson, Deirdre (1978) "Les Ironies comme mentions," *Poétique*, 36, 399-412.

Stackelberg, Jürgen von (1972) *Literarische Rezeptionsformen: Übersetzung, Supplement, Parodie*. Frankfurt: Athenäum.

Steinberg, Leo (1978) "The Glorious Company," in Lipman and Marshall (1978), 8-31.

Sterne, Laurence (1967) *The Life and Opinions of Tristram Shandy, Gentleman*, ed. Graham Petrie. Harmondsworth: Penguin.

Stewart, Susan (1978, 1979) *Nonsense: Aspects of Intertextuality in Folklore and Literature*. Baltimore, Md: Johns Hopkins University Press.

Stierle, Karlheinz (1983) "Werk und Intertextualität," in Schmid and Stempel (1983), 7-26.

Stone, Christopher (1914) *Parody*. London: Martin Secker.

Stoppard, Tom (1967) *Rosencranz and Guildenstern Are Dead*. London: Faber & Faber.

——— (1975) *Travesties*, London: Faber & Faber.

Sturrock, John (1979) "Introduction" to John Sturrock (ed.), *Structuralism and Since*. London: Oxford University Press.

Sühnel, R. (1965) "Satire/Parodie," in *Das Fischer Lexikon: Literatur*, II, 2, 507-19. Frankfurt: Fischer.

Sukenick, Ronald (1975) "Twelve Digressions toward a Study of Composition," *New Literary History*, 6, 429-37.

Svevo, Italo (1930) *The Confessions of Zeno*, trans. Beryl de Zoete. New York: Random House.

Tamke, Alexander (1967) "Jacob Barnes' 'Biblical Name': Central Irony in *The Sun Also Rises*," *The English Record*, 7, 2-7.

Tatham, Campbell (1977) "Mythotherapy and Postmodern Fictions: Magic is Afoot," in Benamou and Carmello (1977), 137-57.

Thomas, D. M. (1981) *The White Hotel*. Harmondsworth: Penguin.

Todorov, Tzvetan (1965) *Théorie de la littérature*, ed. and trans. Tzvetan Todorov. Paris: Seuil.

────── (1978a) *Les Genres du discours*. Paris: Seuil.

────── (1978b) *Symbolisme et interprétation*. Paris: Seuil.

────── (1979) "Bakhtine et l'altérité," *Poétique*, 40, 502-13.

────── (1981) *Mikhail Bakhtine: le principe dialogique*. Paris: Seuil.

Tomachevski, B. (1965) "Thématique," in Todorov (1965), 263-307.

Toulmin, Stephen (1982) "The Construal of Reality: Criticism in Modern and Postmodern Science," *Critical Inquiry*, 9, 93-111.

Treglown, Jeremy (1973) "The Satirical Inversion of Some English Sources in Rochester's Poetry," *Review of English Studies*, 24, 42-8.

Tuve, Rosamond (1970) "Sacred 'Parody' of Love Poetry, and Herbert," in *Essays by Rosamond Tuve: Spenser, Herbert, Milton*, 207-51. Princeton, NJ: Princeton University Press.

Tynjanov, Jurij (1978a) "On Literary Evolution," in Matejka and Pomorska (1978), 66-78.

────── (1978b) "Rhythm as the Constructive Factor of Verse," in Matejka and Pomorska (1978), 126-35.

Valle-Killeen, Suzanne Dolores (1980) *The Satiric Perspective*. New York: Senda Nueva.

van Dijk, Teun A. (1977) *Text and Context*. London and New York: Longman.

Verweyen, Theodor (1973) *Eine Theorie der Parodie*. Munich: Fink.

────── (1979) *Die Parodie in der neueren deutschen Literatur*. Darmstadt: Wissenschaftliche Buchgesellschaft.

Vodička, Felix (1964) "The History of the Echo of Literary Works," *A Prague School Reader on Esthetics, Literary Structure, and Style*, trans. and ed. Paul L. Garvin, 71-81. Washington, DC: Georgetown University Press.

Vossius (1978) "Rhétorique de l'ironie," *Poétique*, 36, 495-508.

Warning, Rainer (1979) "Pour une pragmatique du discours fictionnel," *Poétique*, 39, 321-37.

Watson, Ian (1973) *The Embedding*. New York: Scribner.

Watt, Ian (1966) *The Rise of the English Novel*. Harmondsworth: Penguin.

Weinbrot, Howard D. (1964) "Parody as Imitation in the 18th Century," *American Notes and Queries*, 2, 131-4.

Weisgerber, Jean (1970) "The Use of Quotation in Recent Literature," *Comparative Literature*, 22, 36-45.

Weisstein, Ulrich (1966) "Parody, Travesty, and Burlesque: Imitations with a Vengeance," in François Jost (ed.), *Proceedings of the IVth Congress of the International Comparative Literature Association*, II, 802-11. The Hague: Mouton.

―――― (1970-1) "*The Lonely Baal:* Brecht's First Play as a Parody of Hanns Johst's *Der Einsame,*" *Modern Drama,* 13, 284-303.

Wells, Carolyn (1919) "Parody as a Fine Art," in C. Wells (ed.), *A Parody Anthology,* New York: Scribner.

Whitehead, John (1973) *This Solemn Mockery: The Art of Literary Forgery.* London: Arlington.

Wilde, Alan (1981) *Horizons of Assent: Modernism, Postmodernism, and the Ironic Imagination.* Baltimore, Md: Johns Hopkins University Press.

Wilson, Angus (1967) *No Laughing Matter.* Harmondsworth: Penguin.

Wimsatt, W. K. (1967) *The Verbal Icon.* Lexington, Ky: University of Kentucky Press.

Worchester, David (1940) *The Art of Satire.* Cambridge, Mass.: Harvard University Press.

Wunderlich, Dieter (1971) "Pragmatik, Sprechsituation, Deixis," *Zeitschrift für Literaturwissenschaft und Linguistik,* 1, 153-90.

Yunck, J. A. (1963) "The Two Faces of Parody," *Iowa English Yearbook,* 8, 29-37.

Zima, Peter V. (1981) "Text and Context: The Socio-Linguistic Nexus," in Peter V. Zima (ed.), *Semiotics and Dialectics,* 103-35. Amsterdam: John Benjamins.

Zumthor, Paul (1976) "Le Carrefour des rhétoriqueurs: intertextualité et rhétorique," *Poétique,* 27, 317-37.

INDEX

Abastado, Claude, 18
Acconci, Vito, 13
Adorno, Theodor, 109
Aeschylus, parody of work of, 6
Albalat, Antoine, 37
Albertsen, L.L., 38
Alighieri, Dante, 5, 6, 14, 45, 88, 98, 110-11
Alleman, Beda, 52, 54
Allen, Woody, 18, 25-6, 62, 110
allusion, 6, 25, 34, 42-3, 45, 50, 53, 95, 99, 109
Almansi, Guido, 54
Altmann, Peter, 8
Amis, Kingsley, 4
Amossy, Ruth and Rosen, Elisheva, 38
Antin, David, 111
antiphrasis, see irony
Antonioni, Michelangelo, 106
Apollinaire, Guillaume, 45
Apple, Max, 46
Aquin, Hubert, 82
Arakawa, Shusaku, 8, 9, 10
architecture, parody in, see Post-Modern architecture
Ariosto, Ludovico, 60
Aristophanes, 94
Aristotle, 12, 55
Arnold, Graham, 8
Arnold, Matthew, 69, 77, 80-1, 91
Atwood, Margaret, 81-2
Auden, W.H., 51
Auerbach, Erich, 70
Austen, Jane, 11, 44, 78-9, 91, 96
auto-referentiality, see self-reflexivity
avant-garde, 5, 72, 77, 96

Bach, Johann Sebastian, parodies of work of, 1, 12, 22, 42, 102
Bacon, Francis, 35, 62, 91, 92
Bakhtin, Mikhail, 8, 22, 26, 27, 40-1, 60, 69-83, 95, 103, 109; see also carnivalesque
|Bakhtin, Mikhail|/Vološinov, V.N., 72, 109
Banville, John, 11, 26
Barber, Bruce Alistair, 13, 107
Barth, John, 8, 31, 35, 67, 72
Barthelme, Donald, 46
Barthes, Roland, 4, 11, 26, 37, 75, 76, 85, 90
Bartók, Bela, 35, 40
Bate, W. Jackson, 4
Bauerle, Ruth, 14
Beerbohm, Max, 6, 26, 38, 51, 56-7
Beethoven, Ludwig van, parodies of work of, 8, 39, 42
Belsey, Catherine, 92
Bely, Andrei, parody of work of, 15
Benamou, Michel, 73, 99
Ben-Porat, Ziva, 43, 49, 50
Benstock, Shari, 18, 88
Benton, Robert, 11
Berg, Alban, 22
Berio, Luciano, 22, 42, 60
Bernadac, Marie-Laure, 64
Berto, Giuseppe, 97-8
Bethea, David H. and Davydov, Sergei, 101
biblical parody, 2, 44, 62-3, 73, 74, 75, 80
Bilous, Daniel, 38
Blackmur, Richard P., 43
Blake, Peter, 13